William Henry Husk

Songs of the nativity

Being Christmas carols, ancient and modern

William Henry Husk

Songs of the nativity
Being Christmas carols, ancient and modern

ISBN/EAN: 9783741191893

Manufactured in Europe, USA, Canada, Australia, Japa

Cover: Foto ©Andreas Hilbeck / pixelio.de

Manufactured and distributed by brebook publishing software (www.brebook.com)

William Henry Husk

Songs of the nativity

SONGS OF THE NATIVITY.

Songs of the Nativity;

BEING CHRISTMAS CAROLS,

ANCIENT AND MODERN.

SEVERAL OF WHICH APPEAR FOR THE FIRST TIME
IN A COLLECTION.

EDITED, WITH NOTES, BY

WILLIAM HENRY HUSK,

LIBRARIAN TO THE SACRED HARMONIC
SOCIETY.

LONDON:
JOHN CAMDEN HOTTEN,
74, PICCADILLY.

CHISWICK PRESS:—PRINTED BY WHITTINGHAM AND WILKINS,
TOOKS COURT, CHANCERY LANE.

INTRODUCTION.

HRISTMAS!—What a multitude of associations crowd into the mind at the mere sight or mention of that word! In imagination we are transported to the stable in Bethlehem, and see the Virgin Mother clasping to her breast the Infant Saviour, whilst closer and closer towards the cattle creeps she, in hopes of receiving warmth from their breaths; for, notwithstanding what geographers tell us of the perennial mildness of the climate of Judea, we cannot shake off the belief that

> "It was the winter wild,
> While the Heaven-born child,
> All meanly wrapt in the rude manger lies."

We behold the shepherds in the field, watching their flocks by night—we gaze upon the Angelic vision—we listen to the "good tidings of great joy," and are raised to ecstacy by the celestial chorus—the *first Christmas carol*, as Bishop Jeremy Taylor appropriately styled it,—"Glory to God in the highest, and on earth peace, good will toward men." Our thoughts turn next to the star-led Magi and their offerings to the Holy Child—a feeling of horror overcomes us as we think of the fearful outcry in Bethlehem, the moans of slaughtered Innocents, and the wail-

INTRODUCTION.

ings of bereaved mothers weeping for their children, and refusing to be comforted because they were not, mingling with the savage exclamations of the ferocious soldiery, the instruments of the brutal Herod's cruelty;—but we breathe freely again when we consider that the bloodshed was in vain;—that the tyrant's ends were frustrated, and the Holy Family safe in Egypt.

How many quaint and curious legendary notions—superstitions if you will, but harmless enough in themselves, and frequently of most poetic beauty,—obtained credence with our forefathers in connection with the holy time of celebrating the Nativity! It was believed in the western parts of Devonshire " that at twelve o'clock at night on Christmas Eve the oxen in their stalls were always found on their knees as in an attitude of devotion." Bees were believed to sing in their hives at the same time, and bread baked on Christmas Eve never turned mouldy. In an old print (at the head of a sheet of carols published in 1701) representing the stable at Bethlehem with the Holy Family, figures of an ox, a cow, a sheep, a raven, and a cock are introduced, having labels with Latin inscriptions in their mouths, which are thus explained:—" The cock croweth, *Christus natus est* (Christ is born); the raven asketh, *Quando?* (When?); the cow replieth, *Hac nocte* (This night); the ox crieth out, *Ubi? ubi?* (Where? where?); the sheep bleateth out, *Bethlehem.*"

The crowing of the cock at the approach and break of day has supplied the groundwork of many an old-world fable. It was said that it was about the time of cock-crowing when our Saviour was born; and it was also about that time when He rose from the dead. The spirits of the departed were supposed to possess the power of revisiting the earth during the hours of darkness, but to be compelled to retire at cock-crow. This belief is thus ex-

INTRODUCTION.

pressed by the mighty master of the human heart, Shakspere:—

> "I have heard,
> The cock, that is the trumpet to the morn,
> Doth with his lofty and shrill sounding throat
> Awake the god of day; and at his warning
> The extravagant and erring spirit hies
> To his confine."

And then, in a strain of the loftiest poetry, he proceeds to make us acquainted with a piece of folk-lore so singularly beautiful that we almost feel it difficult to refuse it our belief:—

> "Some say, that ever 'gainst that season comes
> Wherein our Saviour's birth is celebrated,
> The bird of dawning singeth all night long;
> And then, they say, no spirit can walk abroad;
> The nights are wholesome; then no planets strike,
> No fairy takes, nor witch hath power to charm,
> So hallowed and so gracious is the time."

Of the superstitions connected with, and the customs peculiar to, Christmas, a volume might easily be written. To attempt to describe them here would be in vain; we must therefore be content with a few passing notices of some of them, more particularly those which either have within our own time grown, or are fast growing, into disuse.

Concerning Christmas customs as existing in feudal times, we are fortunate in possessing a most graphic description from the pen of one whose admiration of the brighter side of the feudal system with its picturesque and striking features was very great. It embodies in a brief space so many of the customs of the times that, notwithstanding its familiarity, we cannot forbear again quoting it:—

INTRODUCTION.

" Domestic and religious rite
Gave honour to the holy night.
On Christmas Eve the bells were rung;
On Christmas Eve the mass was sung;
That only night, in all the year,
Saw the stoled priest the chalice rear;
The damsel donned her kirtle sheen;
The hall was dressed with holly green;
Forth to the wood did merry men go,
To gather in the mistletoe.
Then opened wide the baron's hall
To vassal, tenant, serf, and all;
Power laid his rod of rule aside,
And ceremony doff'd his pride.
The heir, with roses in his shoes,
That night might village partner choose.
The lord, underogating, share
The vulgar game of "post and pair."
All hailed with uncontroll'd delight
And general voice, the happy night
That to the cottage, as the crown,
Brought tidings of salvation down.
The fire with well dried logs supplied,
Went roaring up the chimney wide;
The huge hall table's oaken face,
Scrubb'd till it shone, the day to grace,
Bore then upon its massive board
No mark to part the squire and lord.
Then was brought in the lusty brawn,
By old, blue-coated serving-man;
Then the grim boar's head frowned on high,
Crested with bays and rosemary.
Well can the green-garb'd ranger tell,
How, when, and where, the monster fell;
What dogs before his death he tore,
And all the baiting of the boar.
The wassail round in good brown bowls,

INTRODUCTION.

> Garnished with ribbon, blithely trowls.
> There the huge sirloin reek'd : hard by
> Plum-porridge stood, and Christmas pie ;
> Nor failed old Scotland to produce
> At such high tide her savoury goose.
> Then came the merry masquers in,
> And carols roar'd with blithesome din ;
> If unmelodious was the song,
> It was a hearty note, and strong.
> Who lists may in their mumming see
> Traces of ancient mystery;
> White shirts supplied the masquerade,
> And smutted cheeks the visor made ;
> But oh! what masquers, richly dight,
> Can boast of bosoms half so light!
> England was merry England when
> Old Christmas brought his sports again.
> 'Twas Christmas broached the mightiest ale,
> 'Twas Christmas told the merriest tale ;
> A Christmas gambol oft would cheer
> A poor man's heart through half the year."*

Whose heart has not bounded with delight on seeing a group of children, newly released from the trammels of the school, returning home to enjoy their Christmas holiday? Listen to the eagerness and the earnestness and glee with which the boys indulge in anticipations of the various pleasures to come ;—the plum-puddings to be made of unusual dimensions,—the new bats and balls or other toys,—the gaily coloured prints adorning the Christmas volumes,—the pantomimes they hope to see—ay, the pantomimes! And here comes one of the Christmas customs which have in our own time flourished in their greatest vigour, and yet seem hastening to decay. Many of us remember the

* Scott's *Marmion.*

INTRODUCTION.

time—it is not so very far distant—when no London theatrical manager ever dreamed of opening his doors at Christmas without placing before his visitors "a new grand comic Christmas pantomime, which has been in preparation *all the summer*." And then the joy of the children as they witnessed the representation. Leigh Hunt, in one of his pleasant papers, says of holiday children:—" But oh, the rapture when the pantomime commences ! Ready to leap out of the box, they joy in the mischief of the clown, laugh at the thwacks he gets for his meddling, and feel no small portion of contempt for his ignorance in not knowing that hot water will scald and gunpowder explode ; whilst with head aside to give fresh energy to the strokes, they ring their little palms against each other in testimony of exuberant delight." The clown is indeed the boys' prime source of enjoyment in a pantomime— the little girls, as their " bringings-up" may have been in the open and honest, or in the straight-laced, school, differ in their estimation of the clown as being very comical, or as dreadfully vulgar, and they either smile or look grave accordingly—but the boys never mince the matter ; they give unrestrained utterance to their gratification. The late Alfred Bunn, in his entertaining work on the Stage, expresses well the feelings which the remembrance of such boyish enjoyments awakes in later life. " Our recollections of, and associations with, Christmas," says he, " and consequently, of and with Grimaldi, are amongst the earliest and happiest of our thoughts. We can never forget our burst of enjoyment on catching the first accents of that many-toned voice, and the first glimpse of that party-coloured face, when, year after year, we have squeezed into any part of the theatre his attraction had left standing room in. Has there been any social happiness of after days the memory of which can impart such true delight,

INTRODUCTION.

as a recurrence to those green and bright hours of life's unclouded boyhood?" All living who can remember the London theatres during the first twenty years or so of the present century agree in bearing testimony to the wonderful powers of Grimaldi as Clown. Those who recollect him are reluctant to admit that any of his successors had any merit; but we cannot refuse our meed of approbation to the talents of Paulo, Tom Matthews, and Flexmore, each in his way an artist. It would be unfair too to pass over the name of the greatest of living clowns, Charles Leclerque, whose dry, quaint humour, and "mute eloquence" are in our opinion unrivalled. But, great as are his abilities, he has latterly had but small chance of displaying them, seeing that at the theatre to which he has been principally attached pantomime has lately been made, as at the majority of our theatres, to give way to that species of extravaganza, miscalled burlesque, in which wit and humour are dispensed with, and the greatest ambition of the author appears to be to display his skill in the distortion in every possible manner of the English vocabulary, and the manufactory of some such *funny* saying as that " a Christmas *carol* will make old *Care howl.*" Let us, however, yet hope that the reign of such dull and senseless absurdities is nearly at an end, and that the taste for the good old-fashioned laughter-provoking pantomime will soon revive, for we cannot believe that it is really defunct. There are still some managers who cling to pantomime, and their crowded houses for weeks after Christmas are sufficient to show that a large portion of the public still prefers the old Christmas fare. Long may their houses continue crowded; and let those who can enjoy the artless, unrestrained mirth of children, attend a morning performance of a pantomime —one of the happiest of modern theatrical ideas—and listen to

INTRODUCTION.

the joyous, ringing laughter of the merry urchins who on such occasions form the vast majority of the auditory.

Another Christmas custom fast approaching to extinction is that of giving Christmas-boxes. Formerly nearly every person who had, or was supposed to have, rendered services to another during the year, looked for a gratuity at Christmas, and in many cases it was regarded almost as a right. Domestic servants in this way levied contributions on the tradesmen who supplied their masters; bankers' clerks received donations from the customers; the clerks and managers of retail traders expected presents from the wholesale dealers, and some even went so far as to convey more than a gentle hint when the proffered gift was of less value than what they conceived themselves "entitled to." Every householder was duly waited on by the postmen (general and twopenny—as the local postmen were called, from the rate of postage charged for the conveyance of letters from one part of the town to another, ere the universal penny post system was established); the lamplighter, the waits, the turncock, the parish beadle, the dustman, the parish watchman (prior to the introduction of the present system of police), and others. A practice existed of tallow-chandlers distributing to the children of their customers, on their applying for them, tiny coloured candles in miniature candlesticks made of bright tin, and it was an amusing sight, as you passed a tallow-chandler's shop on "Boxing-day," to see the crowd of eager urchins, many of whom, like some of their elders, were ready enough to prefer claims having no just foundation, besieging the door, and only prevented from making a forcible entry, *en masse,* into the shop, by the presence of a shopman armed with a long whip. The contentions for precedence, the struggles to get nearest the door, the envious looks

INTRODUCTION.

with which some fortunate recipient of the coveted gift was regarded by his unsuccessful rivals, and other incidents proving the truth of the saying that "the boy is father to the man" were perhaps as instructive as amusing. "A heavy blow and great discouragement" to the custom of Christmas-boxing amongst tradesmen has been given by the growing practice of keeping the shops closed on Boxing-day. Amongst the few persons who still adhere to the old custom are the postmen; and on no one is the gratuity more readily and cheerfully bestowed than on these most useful, hardworked, and underpaid public servants. The dustmen still in many places ask the accustomed benevolence in a most original style. As Christmas draws nigh they distribute a hand-bill preferring their petition. Here is a copy of one of the last year circulated in one of the wealthiest metropolitan parishes:—

"To the Worthy Inhabitants of St. George's, Westminster.

"Ladies and Gentlemen,—We, the regular DUSTMEN of this Parish, in the employ of John Baldwin & Co. make humble application to you for a CHRISTMAS BOX, which you are usually so kind in giving. We bring our token, which consists of a handsome and antique Silver Medal, commemorating the peace of Luneville, when the combined forces fought against the great Napoleon in Belgium. The figures represent 'Peace,' with her olive branch and horn of plenty, leading 'Industry,' who is seated on her car, drawn by two lions; the inscription is—' Stets Leite sie Friede,' signifying—Lead her always in Peace. Dated—Luneville, D. 9 Februar, 1801. On the reverse side is the figure of a man half reclining, as though awoke from slumber, holding a reed in one hand, the other extended appealingly to the heavens; inscription—' Wann tagts auch hier,' signifying—

INTRODUCTION.

When breaks the daylight here. At the bottom is the name Abramson. No connexion with Scavengers.

"CHRISTOPHER MAJOR. JAMES OLIVER.

"Caution.—There being persons who go about with the intent to defraud us, and impose on you, be so kind as not to give your bounty to any person who cannot produce a Medal as above. Please not to return this bill."

One is puzzled which to admire most in this production;—the elaborate description of the "antique" medal, (which, we suppose, must be in some way or another, although perhaps remotely, connected with the dustman's vocation, although our limited capacity does not permit us to perceive it), or the simplicity and candour which shows us that the offence of "defrauding us" is in the writer's mind a graver one than that of "imposing on you."

Another functionary, who still expects his "Christmas-box," is the Parish-beadle, who, in the exercise of his duty, has to distribute amongst the inhabitants about Christmastide a broad sheet containing a list of the parish officers for the year, with other information, and who at the same time leaves on his own account another broadside containing "A copy of Verses for 18—! humbly presented to all my worthy Masters and Mistresses in the Parish of St. ———, ——— ———, by ———, ———, Beadle and Bellman." This sheet is surrounded by woodcuts; that at the top representing the "Beadle and Bellman" accompanied by watchmen or others, and the remainder generally representing various incidents in the life of our Saviour. The verses are usually on the Nativity, and other festivals occurring at Christmastide; addresses "to my Masters and Mistresses," "the Young Men," "the Young Maidens,"

INTRODUCTION.

and the like, with, occasionally, one on some unusual occurrence within the expiring year. The following lines which a newly-appointed Beadle thought fit [in 1834] to insert in memory of his predecessor afford a fair sample of the "poetry" of these worthies:—

" ON THE LATE BEADLE.
" Since our good friend is gone to rest
Within the silent grave ;
We hope his soul is 'mongst the blest,—
Let fruitless sorrows waive."

The custom of distributing these verses is a very old one, and one printing office,—that of Messrs. Reynell, formerly of Piccadilly, and now of Little Pulteney-street—has continuously enjoyed the distinction of printing for many of the London beadles since the year 1735. Why the metropolitan "Bumbles" are so constant in their patronage of this establishment we know not. Can it be that they find a poet as well as a typographer on the premises ?

The custom of the company assembled to celebrate Twelfth-night supporting assumed characters seems, judging from the absence from the pastrycooks' windows of the sheets on which the coloured representations of such characters were printed, to have passed away. The selection, by lot, of a king and queen to preside over the Twelfth-night festivities is very ancient, and the addition of other characters generally representing the courtiers, though not unfrequently others, and often the chief personages of some popular comedy, dates back at least two centuries. The names of these characters were written on slips of paper which were put into the cake. In 1669 this practice was abandoned, and the names were drawn from a hat. Towards

INTRODUCTION.

the latter end of the last century pictorial representations of the characters were introduced. These were of the invention of John Britton, the topographer and antiquary, and some of the earliest of them were drawn and engraved by the elder Cruikshank. It is not unlikely that the latter's son, the admirable artist, George Cruikshank, still amongst us, may have witnessed, during his long life, the rise, general prevalence, gradual decay, and perhaps total extinction of the custom of using these character-pictures.

What school-boy of the present day knows anything of CHRISTMAS-PIECES? We mean not pantomimes, extravaganzas, or any other species of theatrical entertainment, but specimens of handwriting which were carefully prepared under the superintendence of the writing-master, in all schools immediately before the breaking-up for the Christmas vacation, in order to manifest to the "parents and guardians" the improvement made during the year by the pupils in the caligraphic art. These "pieces" were on large sheets of writing paper of the size known as "imperial," spread open. They were bordered by engravings, the space in the centre being reserved for the writing. A very extensive collection of "pieces," comprising an almost unbroken series from the year 1720 until about 1840, lies before the writer at the time of writing. The engravings, which in the earlier pieces are of considerable merit, but which became by degrees poorer and poorer, consist of representations of some important event which had happened during the year, such as battles by land or sea, the earthquake at Lisbon, the coronation of George III, and the like; or scenes illustrating "Rural sports," "Summer diversions," "Bartholomew fair," Military exercises, &c. Scripture subjects were sometimes (although by

INTRODUCTION.

no means frequently) introduced. About 1805 the practice of colouring the engravings commenced and slowly gained ground until about 1820, when it became universal. From about the latter date, too, the engravings were almost exclusively confined to Scripture subjects. From the period of the introduction of colour the engravings rapidly deteriorated, passing from a respectable kind of copper-plate, through various phases of outlines, serving merely as a guide to the colourist, until they terminated in wood-cuts of the coarsest and commonest description. For many years prior to their ceasing to be published, the use of these Christmas pieces had been discontinued in respectable schools on account of an objectionable practice which prevailed of the boys in the parochial schools and lower class of private schools going about from house to house exhibiting their pieces as a means of obtaining " Christmas-boxes." Formerly the writing of " pieces" was not confined to Christmas, but was also used in some schools at Whitsuntide.

We have yet to speak of one other departing Christmas custom—that of singing Carols. Although once so universally prevalent throughout the entire length and breadth of the land as to warrant the assumption that it was permanently rooted in the habits of the people, this interesting custom has been for a long time on the wane. Fifty years ago carols were beginning " to be spoken of as not belonging to this century ;"—thirty years back they were said to be " still sung during the festive season in many parts of the country, though now seldom heard in the metropolis." This latter is perhaps to some extent still the case. Generally speaking, however, it may be said that the printers of sheet carols resident in London, who formerly supplied a considerable number of country dealers, now issue but few carols at

INTRODUCTION.

Christmas-tide; and the country printers, although the sheets published by them as collections of carols contain a much larger number of pieces than those put forth by their metropolitan brethren, find the taste of their customers rather incline towards hymns, mostly those in use amongst dissenting congregations, than to the genuine Christmas carol, and they suit them accordingly. Such carols as are still printed by these popular typographers and publishers are mentioned in the notes on the following collection. The old festive carol seems to have grown into almost total neglect. A certain section of the clergy, anxious for the conservation of old customs, particularly of those associated with the great Church festivals, have occasionally, during the last twenty or thirty years, made attempts to revive a taste for the use of Christmas carols amongst their parishioners. But their efforts have been too intermittent and spasmodic to produce any successful result, and they seem also to have forgotten that no custom can be either established, sustained, or revived by the mere desire of persons in authority. Unless the free spontaneous wish of the people shall concur to give it vitality, it will soon droop and die. The practice of carol-singing, however, may yet revive. Many amongst us remember, more than forty years since, a popular song, entitled, "The Good old days of Adam and Eve," in which the singer recalled to memory many things then passed away, amongst them the time

> "When Christmas had its Christmas carols,
> And ladies' sides were hooped like barrels."

As we have seen the latter custom return and maintain itself for several years, we may also live to see the former resume all its pristine vigour.

Perhaps the greatest characteristic of Christmas Day at pre-

INTRODUCTION.

sent is the very general custom of regarding it as a domestic and family festival. The thoughts of men seem to turn on that day more especially towards home and kindred, and members of families who have during the rest of the year been scattered assemble together at the table of the head of the family. Children, joyous children, fresh from school, form a part, by no means the least interesting, of the happy circle, which is perhaps completed by the addition of some old and valued friend, it may be the school companion of the host or hostess. Although many of the old sports and pastimes, once inseparable from such a Christmas party, may be no longer resorted to, nor many of the old Christmas customs observed, yet there is no lack of cheerfulness and even merriment; and one of the chief sources of amusement is the telling, hearing, or reading of the Christmas manners, habits, and customs of bygone times.

It is hoped, therefore, that it may not be deemed presumptuous to suppose that the present volume will be not unwelcome to such a circle of readers and listeners.

It has been compiled—not for the purpose of forming a complete and exhaustive collection of Christmas carols; for that would not only have swollen it to unwieldy dimensions, but have necessitated the introduction of numerous pieces of very inferior character, but—in order, by placing before the reader a selection of all the choicest productions of the kind, both ancient and modern, to show what Christmas carols were and are. The materials for it have been drawn from the most extensive and varied sources; ancient manuscripts, early printed books, rare musical works, old almanacs, and, in no small degree, the common broadsides, those remarkable productions of the cheap printing press, which have been the means of preserving to us no inconsiderable

INTRODUCTION.

number of the pieces still extant in this particular walk of literature.

The carols here given were produced at various times extending over a period of nearly five hundred years. Care has been taken in selecting them to observe impartiality between the old and the new;—the productions of the remote past, and those of times nearer to our own,—so that the book shall present a fair specimen of both without exhibiting an undue preference for either. Many of the pieces, and some of them not the least in point of literary merit, are introduced into a collection of carols for the first time; others, which have already appeared in collections, have been collated with, and corrected by, the original or other early printed copies. The spelling of the older carols has been modernised, but no other material alteration made. The carols are arranged under two heads, *Religious Carols*, including all those of a legendary character, as well as those relating to Scripturally recorded events, and *Festive Carols and Songs*, comprising productions of a more secular kind.

In conclusion, the Editor ventures to express a hope that the volume may find favour in the sight of his fellow-countrymen and country-women, and contribute in some degree to their enjoyment of "A MERRIE CHRISTMAS."

W. H. H.

CHRISTMAS CAROLS.

PART I.

RELIGIOUS CAROLS.

"His place of birth, a solemn Angel tells
To simple shepherds, keeping watch by night;
They gladly thither haste, and by a quire
Of squadron'd Angels hear His *carol* sung."
                                    MILTON.

A CAROL FOR CHRISTMAS EVE.

This seems peculiar to the West-country. It was printed by Davies Gilbert in his collection of " Ancient Christmas Carols, with the tunes to which they were formerly sung in the West of England;" first published in 1822. The carols in that collection, Mr. Gilbert says, were chanted in churches on Christmas day, and in private houses on Christmas eve, throughout the West of England, up to the latter part of the late century. He adds: " Christmas Day, like every other great festival, has prefixed to it in the Calendar a Vigil or Fast; and in Catholic countries Mass is still celebrated at midnight after Christmas Eve, when austerities cease, and rejoicings of all kinds succeed. Shadows of these customs were, till very lately, preserved in the Protestant West of England. The day of Christmas Eve was passed in an ordinary manner; but at seven or eight o'clock in the evening cakes were drawn hot from the oven; cyder or beer exhilarated the spirits in every house; and the singing of carols was continued late into the night. On Christmas Day these carols took the place of psalms in all the Churches, especially at afternoon service, the whole congregation joining; and at the end it was usual for the parish clerk to declare, in a loud voice, his wishes for a merry Christmas and a happy New Year to all the parishioners." Rude though it be, the simplicity and earnestness of this carol render it very characteristic and pleasing.

HE Lord at first did Adam make
Out of the dust and clay,
And in his nostrils breathed life,
E'en as the Scriptures say.
And then in Eden's Paradise
He placed him to dwell,

RELIGIOUS CAROLS.

That he within it should remain
  To dress and keep it well.
    Now let good Christians all begin
      An holy life to live,
    And to rejoice and merry be,
      For this is Christmas Eve.

And then within the garden he
  Commanded was to stay,
And unto him in commandment
  These words the Lord did say:
" The fruit which in the garden grows
  To thee shall be for meat,
Except the tree in the midst thereof,
  Of which thou shalt not eat."
    Now let good Christians, &c.

" For in the day that thou shalt eat,
  Or do it then come nigh;
For if that thou doth eat thereof
  Then surely thou shalt die."
But Adam he did take no heed
  Unto that only thing,
But did transgress God's holy law,
  And so was wrapt in sin.
    Now let good Christians, &c.

Now mark the goodness of the Lord
  Which He for mankind bore;
His mercy soon He did extend,
  Lost man for to restore;

RELIGIOUS CAROLS.

And then for to redeem our souls
   From death and hellish thrall,
He said His own dear Son should be
   The Saviour of us all.
      Now let good Christians, &c.

Which promise now is brought to pass,
   Christians, believe it well;
And by the coming of God's dear Son
   We are redeemed from thrall.
Then if we truly do believe,
   And do the thing aright;
Then by His merits we at last
   Shall live in heaven bright.
      Now let good Christians, &c.

Now for the blessings we enjoy,
   Which are from heaven above,
Let us renounce all wickedness
   And live in perfect love.
Then shall we do Christ's own command,
   Ev'n His own written word;
And when we die in heaven shall
   Enjoy our living Lord.
      Now let good Christians, &c.

And now the tide is nigh at hand
   In which our Saviour came;
Let us rejoice and merry be
   In keeping of the same.

RELIGIOUS CAROLS.

Let's feed the poor and hungry souls
And such as do it crave;
Then when we die in heaven sure
Our reward we shall have.

Now let good Christians all begin
An holy life to live,
And to rejoice and merry be,
For this is Christmas Eve.

WELCOME, YULE.

YULE, it is almost needless to observe, is the Anglo-Saxon name for Christmas. This carol is found in a manuscript of the time of Henry VI. preserved in the British Museum, but there is no doubt that the composition is of much earlier date.

The enumeration of the various festivals which occur during the period of Yule-tide, which lasted until Candlemas day, is found in other carols beside the present. Thomas the Martyr mentioned in the second stanza was Thomas à Becket, or, as he was more commonly styled, St. Thomas of Canterbury, whose festival was celebrated on the 29th of December.

Welcome, Yule, thou merry man
In worship of this holy day.

ELCOME be thou heaven's King;
Welcome, born in one morning,
Welcome, for whom we shall sing
Welcome, Yule.

RELIGIOUS CAROLS.

Welcome be ye, Stephen and John,
Welcome, Innocents every one,
Welcome, Thomas, Martyr one,
      Welcome, Yule.

Welcome be ye, good New Year,
Welcome, Twelfth day both in fere,[1]
Welcome, Saints loved and dear,
      Welcome, Yule.

Welcome be ye, Candlemass,
Welcome be ye, Queen of Bliss,
Welcome both to more and less,[2]
      Welcome, Yule.

Welcome be ye that are here,
Welcome, all, and make good cheer,
Welcome all, another year,
      Welcome, Yule.

[1] Company.   [2] Great and small.

A YULE-TIDE CAROL.

This carol is contained in the same valuable manuscript as the preceding. Like that it enumerates, but with more particularity, the various festivals celebrated during Yule-tide. There is another copy, slightly differing from the present, in a manuscript of the same age, which was edited by Mr. Thomas Wright for the Percy Society in 1847; and in which the stanza relating to St. Thomas of Canterbury, Mr. Wright tells us, has been blotted out by a later hand. This is not a singular instance of such disfigurement of books containing passages in which " the holy blissful martyr," as Chaucer terms him, was favourably mentioned. That the memory of Thomas à Becket, the sturdy assertor of the supremacy of the spiritual over the temporal power, should be obnoxious to that quondam " Defender of the Faith," Henry VIII, was not unnatural, and it is not surprising he should have used the most persevering efforts to extirpate the reverence in which the people had for ages held the murdered Archbishop, and which had made his shrine at Canterbury the most frequented place of pilgrimage in England. There are still extant many missals and other service books in which the pen has been unsparingly used, not merely in obliterating the name of " St. Thomas of Canterbury " from the calendar, but in blotting out the entire office appointed for his feast day.

    Make we mirth
    For Christ His birth,
    And sing we Yule till Candlemas.

THE first day of Yule we have in mind
How man was born all of our kind,
For He would the bonds unbind
 Of all our sin and wickedness.

RELIGIOUS CAROLS.

The second day we sing of Stephen
That stoned was, and said up even
With Christ there he would stand in heaven,
    And crowned was for his prowess.

The third day 'longs to St. John,
That was Christ's darling, dearest one,
To whom He took, when He should gone,
    His dear mother for his cleanness.

The fourth day of the Children young
With Herod's wrath to death were throng,
Of Christ they could not speak with tongue,
    But with their blood bare witness.

The fifth day hallowed St. Thomas,
Right as strong as pillar of brass,
Held up his church and slain was,
    For he stood fast in righteousness.

The eighth day took Jesu His name,
That saved mankind from sin and shame,
And circumcised was for no blame,
    But for example of meekness.

The twelfth day offered to Him Kings three,
Gold, myrrh, incense, these gifts free,
For God and man and king is He,
    And thus they worshipped his worthiness.

RELIGIOUS CAROLS.

The fortieth day came Mary mild
Unto the Temple with her child,
To shew her clean that never was 'filed,
And herewith ends Christmas.

A CAROL OF THE BIRTH OF CHRIST.

THIS is an ancient carol of rather peculiar construction. It is contained in a manuscript written early in the sixteenth century, which is preserved in the British Museum, and in which it bears the above title. Except in a collection of Specimens of Old Christmas Carols, edited by Mr. Thomas Wright for the Percy Society, this carol has never before been printed.

HE golden time is now at hand,
   The day of joy from heaven doth spring,
Salvation overflows the land,
   Wherefore all faithful thus may sing,
     Glory to God most high,
     And peace on the earth continually,
    And unto men rejoicing!

The birth of Christ who list to hear,
To this our song let them give ear,
   Which shews the same most plainly:
The Angel Gabriel from above
Was sent by God to break His love
   Unto the Virgin Mary;

RELIGIOUS CAROLS.

Who said, "Hail, Mary, full of grace,
Blessed art thou of woman's race,
The Lord is with thee certainly,
As He hath sent thee word by me."
When she heard this she was afraid,
And cast in her mind what he had said;
The Angel said, "Fear not, Mary,
The Son of God doth dwell with thee.

"Lo, in thy womb thou shalt conceive,
And bear a Son whose name shall have
   The glorious name of Jesus;
He shall be great in majesty,
And called the Son of God Most High,
   Who still shall dwell amongst us.
The Lord for Him shall well provide
The seat of His father, David;
And He shall reign for evermore,
A safeguard still unto the poor,
Whose kingdom sure shall have no end,
But still in joys the time to spend."
The Virgin said to th' Angel then,
"How shall this be? I know no man."

The Angel answered and said,
"The Holy Ghost, be not afraid,
   From heaven shall come upon thee;
And by the grace of God Most High,
Power shall overshadow thee,
   I tell the truth, believe me.

RELIGIOUS CAROLS.

And also thy cousin, Elizabeth,
So in like wise conceived hath;
Thus God can make the barren tree
To bud with fruit most pleasantly."
Then Mary said, with one accord,
"Behold the handmaid of the Lord!
The will of God be done in me
As it shall please His majesty!"

When forty weeks were come and gone,
In Bethlehem this our Lord was born,
   As Esay[1] he did prophecy;
The shepherds keeping sheep by night,
The Lord did compass them with light,
   His Angel walking hard by.
The shepherds then were sore dismay'd,
The Angel said, "Be not afraid,
I bring you tidings of such joy
As Satan's force cannot destroy.
For why? to you is born this day
The Saviour of the world, I say:
This is the sign, where you shall see
A swaddled child in manger lie."

The shepherds straight to Bethlehem went,
As they by the Angel then were sent,
   Where Joseph was with Mary;
And as the Angel to them said,

[1] Isaiah.

RELIGIOUS CAROLS.

They found the child in manger laid,
  Whom they did worship truly.
And spread abroad what they did see,
As the Angel told them certainly,
Rejoicing greatly at the same,
And praising God's Most Holy Name,
For sending down His only Son
For our salvation to be born;
Which was as now this Christenmas,
Rejoice, therefore, both more and less.[1]

THE VIRGIN AND CHILD.

THIS carol is contained in a very curious manuscript copy of Songs and Carols, which was edited by Mr. Thomas Wright in 1847 for the Percy Society. The manuscript was, in Mr. Wright's opinion, "written in the latter half of the fifteenth century, probably during the period intervening between the latter end of the reign of Henry VI, and the beginning of that of Henry VII." There is another copy in a manuscript of the same period preserved in the Advocates' Library, Edinburgh. The easy flow of the verse, the grace of expression, and the refinement of the piece generally, are very remarkable, considering the period of production.

HIS endris[2] night
  I saw a sight,
    A star as bright as day;
  And ever among
  A maiden sung,
    Lullay, by by, lullay.

---

[1] Great and small.   [2] Last.

RELIGIOUS CAROLS.

This lovely lady sat and sang, and to her Child said—
" My son, my brother, my father dear, why lyest Thou thus in hayd.[1]
    My sweet bird,
    Thus it is betide
      Though thou be king veray;[2]
    But, nevertheless,
    I will not cease
      To sing, by by, lullay."

The Child then spake in His talking, and to His mother said—
" I bekyd[3] am King, in crib[4] there I be laid;
    For Angels bright
    Down to Me light,
      Thou knowest it is no nay,[5]
    And of that sight
    Thou mayst be light[6]
      To sing, by by, lullay."

" Now, sweet Son, since Thou art King, why art Thou laid in stall?
Why not Thou ordained Thy bedding in some great king his hall?
    Me thinketh it is right
    That king or knight
      Should lie in good array;
    And then among
    It were no wrong
      To sing, by by, lullay."

[1] Winter.   [2] True.   [3] I am renowned as.
[4] Manger.   [5] Not to be denied.   [6] Quick.

RELIGIOUS CAROLS.

"Mary, mother, I am thy child, though I be laid in stall,
Lords and dukes shall worship Me, and so shall kings all;
      Ye shall well see
      That kings three
         Shall come the twelfth day;
      For this behest
      Give me thy breast
         And sing, by by, lullay."

"Now tell me, sweet Son, I Thee pray, Thou art my love and dear,
How should I keep Thee to Thy pay,[1] and make Thee glad of cheer;
      For all Thy will
      I would fulfil
         Thou witest[2] full well in fay,[3]
      And for all this
      I will thee kiss
         And sing, by by, lullay."

"My dear mother, when time it be, thou take Me up aloft,
And set Me upon thy knee, and handle Me full soft;
      And in thy arm
      Thou wilt me warm,
         And keep night and day;
      If I weep
      And may not sleep,
         Thou sing, by by, lullay."

[1] Satisfaction.   [2] Knowest.   [3] Faith.

RELIGIOUS CAROLS.

" Now, sweet Son, since it is so, that all thing is at Thy will,
I pray thee grant me a boon, if it be both right and skill,[1]
   That child or man,
   That will or can
    Be merry upon my day;
   To bliss them bring,
   And I shall sing
    Lullay, by by, lullay."

A CAROL FOR CHRISTMAS DAY.

THIS and the following carol are taken from a rare musical publication bearing the title of " ¶ Songs of sundrie natures, some of grauitie, and others of myrth, fit for all companies and voyces. Lately made and composed into Musicke of 3. 4. 5. and 6. parts: and published for the delight of all such as take pleasure in the exercise of that Art. By William Byrd, one of the Gentlemen of the Queenes Maiesties honorable Chappell. ¶ Imprinted at London by Thomas East, the assigne of William Byrd, and are to be sold at the house of the sayd T. East, being in Aldersgate streete, at the signe of the blacke Horse. 1589. Cum priuilegio Regiæ Maiestatis." Each of the two pieces is designated, " A Carowle for Christmas day." Prior to its publication by Byrd, the present carol had appeared in the collection of poems entitled " The Paradise of Dainty Devices," 1576, with the initials, F. K. (those of Francis Kinwelmersh) attached to it. Both this and the succeeding carol are here given from a copy of Byrd's work in the Library of the Sacred Harmonic Society. Neither has hitherto been reproduced in any collection of carols

     [1] Reasonable.

RELIGIOUS CAROLS.

Rejoice, rejoice, with heart and voice,
In Christ His birth this day rejoice.

ROM Virgin's womb this day did spring
    The precious seed that only saved man,
This day let man rejoice and sweetly sing,
    Since on this day salvation first began.
This day did Christ man's soul from death remove
With glorious Saints to dwell in heaven above.

This day to man came pledge of perfect peace,
    This day to man came love and unity,
This day man's grief began for to surcease,
    This day did man receive a remedy
For each offence and every deadly sin
With guilty heart that erst he wandered in.

In Christ His flock let love be surely placed,
    From Christ His flock let concord hate expel,
Of Christ His flock let love be so embraced,
    As we in Christ and Christ in us may dwell.
Christ is the author of sweet unity,
From whence proceedeth all felicity.

O sing unto this glittering glorious King,
O praise His Name let every living thing,
Let heart and voice like bells of silver ring
The comfort that this day to man doth bring.
Let lute, let shalm, with sound of sweet delight,
These joys of Christ His birth this day recite.

A CAROL FOR CHRISTMAS DAY.

SEE note on the preceding carol.

Cast off all doubtful care,
Exile and banish tears;
To joyful news divine
Lend us your list'ning ears.

AN earthly tree a heavenly fruit it bare,
 A case of clay contained a crown immortal,
 A crown of crowns, a King whose cost and care
  Redeemed poor man, whose race before was thrall
To death, to doom, to pains of everlasting,
By His sweet death, scorns, stripes, and often fasting.

A star above the stars, a sun of light,
 Whose blessed beams this wretched earth bespread
With hope of heaven and of God's Son the sight,
 Which in our flesh and sinful soul lay dead.
O faith, O hope, O joys renowned for ever,
O lively life that deathless shall persever.

RELIGIOUS CAROLS.

Then let us sing the lullabys of sleep
　To this sweet babe, born to awake us all
From drowsy sin that made old Adam weep,
　And by his fault gave to mankind the fall.
For lo! this day, the birth day, day of days,
　Summons our songs to give Him laud and praise.

A CAROL FOR CHRISTMAS DAY.

This appears, under the above name, in William Byrd's " Psalmes, Songs, and Sonnets: some solemne, others ioyfull, framed to the life of the Words: Fit for Voyces or Viols of 3. 4. 5. and 6. Parts," printed at London in 1611, and a copy of which, (whence the present carol has been derived) is in the library of the Sacred Harmonic Society. It has not been included in any collection of carols, and is here given only as a singular specimen of a carol not in rhymed verse.

HIS day Christ was born,
　　This day our Saviour did appear,
　　This day the Angels sing in earth,
　　The Archangels are glad;
This day the just rejoice, saying,
　Glory be to God on high.
　　　ALLELUJAH!

THE SINNER'S REDEMPTION.

THIS is one of the most popular carols. It is annually reprinted by the broadside printers, and is included in most of the existing collections of carols. Possibly the oldest known copy of this carol is that contained in the undated edition of Thomas Deloney, " the ballading silk-weaver's," *Garland of Good Will*, believed to have been issued in 1709. It is there entitled, " The Sinner's Redemption: The Nativity of our Lord and Saviour Jesus Christ, with His life on earth, and precious death on the Cross." Although appearing in that publication there is no reason for supposing it to have been written by Deloney, who died in 1600; but there is no doubt of its being of considerable age. The copy printed in 1709 consists of twenty-eight verses, but wants the burthen, " And to redeem," &c; the last twelve of these verses, however, are commonly omitted, as relating not to the commencement of our blessed Lord's career on earth, but to its conclusion. The shorter version, as being the most generally used, is here retained. In Davies Gilbert's collection the carol commences, " *Let all* that are to mirth inclined;" and there is extant a sheet of music issued by a London publisher (who withheld his name) about 1775, containing a short version of the carol, differing from Gilbert's, but commencing in the same way, set to a tune composed by J. A;—M. B.—possibly John Alcock, organist of Lichfield Cathedral, or his son, John. In a copy in the Roxburgh collection of Ballads the carol is directed to be sung " To the tune of *My bleeding heart*, or, *In Creet*."

LL you that are to mirth inclined,
Consider well and bear in mind
What our good God for us hath done
In sending his beloved Son.
  And to redeem our souls from thrall,
  He[1] is the Saviour of us all.

[1] " Christ" in the West-country version.

RELIGIOUS CAROLS.

Let all your songs and praises be
Unto his Heavenly Majesty,
And evermore among your mirth
Remember Christ our Saviour's birth.
         And to redeem, &c.

The five-and-twentieth of December,
Good cause have you for to remember,
In Bethlehem upon this morn
There was our blessed Saviour born.
         And to redeem, &c.

The night before that happy tide
The spotless Virgin, and her guide,
Went long time seeking up and down,
To find them lodging in the town.
         And to redeem, &c.

And mark how all things came to pass,
The inns and lodgings so filled was,
That they could have no room at all,
But in a silly[1] ox's stall.
         And to redeem, &c.

That night the Virgin Mary mild
Was safe delivered of a Child,
According unto Heaven's decree
Man's sweet salvation for to be.
         And to redeem, &c.

[1] Simple, inoffensive.

RELIGIOUS CAROLS.

Near Bethlehem did Shepherds keep
Their herds and flocks of feeding sheep,
To whom God's Angel did appear,
Which put the Shepherds in great fear.
    And to redeem, &c.

"Prepare and go," the Angel said,
"To Bethlehem, be not afraid;
There shall you see this blessed morn,
The princely babe, sweet Jesus, born."
    And to redeem, &c.

With thankful hearts and joyful mind,
The Shepherds went this Babe to find,
And as the heavenly Angel told,
They did our Saviour Christ behold.
    And to redeem, &c.

Within a manger was he laid,
The Virgin Mary by him stayed,
Attending on the Lord of life,
Being both mother, maid, and wife.
    And to redeem, &c.

Three Eastern Wise Men from afar,
Directed by a glorious Star,
Came boldly on, and made no stay
Until they came where Jesus lay.
    And to redeem, &c.

RELIGIOUS CAROLS.

And being come unto the place
Wherein the blest Messias was,
They humbly laid before his feet
Their gifts of gold and odours sweet.
          And to redeem, &c.

See how the Lord of Heaven and Earth
Shewed himself lowly in his birth,
A sweet example for mankind,
To learn to bear an humble mind.
          And to redeem, &c.

No costly robes or rich attire
Did Jesus Christ our Lord desire.
No music nor sweet harmony,
Till glorious Angels from on high,
          And to redeem, &c.

Did in melodious manner sing
Praises unto our heavenly King;
All honour, glory, might and power
Be unto Christ our Saviour.
          And to redeem, &c.

If choirs of Angels did rejoice,
Well may mankind with heart and voice
Sing praises to the God of Heaven,
That unto us his Son is given.
          And to redeem, &c.

ON CHRISTMAS DAY IN THE MORNING.

This carol enjoys a very extensive popularity. It is found, under various forms, in nearly every collection of sheet carols. One of the most frequently printed versions is entitled, "The Sunny Bank." This is said to be of Warwickshire or Staffordshire origin; but its use is not confined to those, or the neighbouring, counties, as it is printed both in the North and West of England.

The entire carol, omitting the repetitions, which occur precisely as in the carol, "On Christmas Day in the morning," is comprised in the following words:—

"As I sat on a sunny bank
   On Christmas day in the morning,
I spied three ships come sailing by.
And who should be with those three ships
   But Joseph and his fair lady.
O he did whistle and she did sing,
And all the bells on earth did ring
For joy that our Saviour He was born
   On Christmas day in the morning."

There is also a Kentish version which runs thus:—the repetitions being omitted as in the above:—

"As I sat under a sycamore tree,
I looked me out upon the sea
   On Christmas day in the morning.
I saw three ships a sailing there,
The Virgin Mary and Christ they bare.
He did whistle and she did sing,
And all the bells on earth did ring.

RELIGIOUS CAROLS.

And now we hope to taste your cheer,
And wish you all a happy New Year
On Christmas Day in the morning."

For an explanation of how the *two* holy persons named in these carols contrived to occupy *three* ships we must refer either to the expounders of miracles, or to the Court Newsman, who was wont to tell the public that the Queen went in six carriages to the theatre, or elsewhere.

Ritson the antiquary, in the Introduction to his collection of Scottish Songs, gives some lines sung during the Christmas holidays about the middle of the sixteenth century, in which the following stanza occurs:—

" There comes a ship far sailing then,
Saint Michel was the stieres-man;
  Saint John sate in the horn:
Our Lord harped, our Lady saug,
And all the bells of heaven they rang,
  On Christ's Sonday at morn."

This may be the original of the three ships of our carol.

SAW three ships come sailing in,
  On Christmas Day, on Christmas Day:
I saw three ships come sailing in
  On Christmas Day in the morning.

And who was in those ships all three,
  On Christmas Day, on Christmas Day?
And who was in those ships all three,
  On Christmas Day in the morning?

Our Saviour Christ and his lady,
  On Christmas Day, on Christmas Day;
Our Saviour Christ and his lady,
  On Christmas Day in the morning.

RELIGIOUS CAROLS.

Pray whither sailed those ships all three,
On Christmas Day, on Christmas Day?
Pray whither sailed those ships all three,
On Christmas Day in the morning?

O they sailed into Bethlehem,
On Christmas Day, on Christmas Day;
O they sailed into Bethlehem,
On Christmas Day in the morning.

And all the bells on earth shall ring,
On Christmas Day, on Christmas Day;
And all the bells on earth shall ring,
On Christmas Day in the morning.

And all the Angels in heaven shall sing,
On Christmas Day, on Christmas Day;
And all the Angels in heaven shall sing,
On Christmas Day in the morning.

And all the souls on earth shall sing,
On Christmas Day, on Christmas Day;
And all the souls on earth shall sing,
On Christmas Day in the morning.

Then let us all rejoice amain,
On Christmas Day, on Christmas Day;
Then let us all rejoice amain,
On Christmas Day in the morning.

GOD REST YOU, MERRY GENTLEMEN.

There is no carol, perhaps, so universally known as this. Many, who have heard no other carol, are familiar with "God rest you, merry gentlemen," and speak of it as *the* Christmas carol. The only carols which at the present time in any degree approach it in point of popularity are "The Seven Joys," and "The Sunny Bank," which many of the broadside printers annually associate with it on the same sheet; accompanied of late years by an English translation of the Latin Christmas hymn, "Adeste, fideles," under the title of the Portuguese Hymn, or as one worthy printer calls it "A favourite Christmas Hymn, *translated from the Portuguese*," ignorant of the fact that its title of "Portuguese," was given to it by an English nobleman who was a director of the Concerts of Ancient Music and introduced the hymn there, having previously heard it sung at the Chapel of the Portuguese embassy in South Street, Grosvenor Square, and assuming it to be a Portuguese composition. As may be expected of a piece so often printed and sung in districts so widely separated there are several variations in the different copies of this carol, but the version here printed seems the most generally received, and is perhaps the most genuine.

OD rest you, merry gentlemen,
  Let nothing you dismay,
  Remember Christ, our Saviour,
   Was born on Christmas day;
To save us all from Satan's power,
 When we were gone astray.
  O tidings of comfort and joy.

RELIGIOUS CAROLS.

In Bethlehem, in Jewry
   This blessed babe was born,
And laid within a manger
   Upon this blessed morn;
The which His mother Mary
   Did nothing take in scorn.
               O tidings, &c.

From God, our Heavenly Father,
   A blessed Angel came,
And unto certain shepherds,
   Brought tidings of the same;
That there was born in Bethlehem
   The Son of God by name.
               O tidings, &c.

" Fear not," then said the Angel,
   " Let nothing you affright,
" For there is born in Bethlehem
   " Of a pure Virgin bright,
" One able to advance you,
   " And throw down Satan quite."
               O tidings, &c.

The shepherds, at those tidings,
   Rejoiced much in mind,
And left their flocks a-feeding
   In tempest, storm, and wind,
And straightway went to Bethlehem
   The Son of God to find.
               O tidings, &c.

RELIGIOUS CAROLS.

But when they came to Bethlehem,
  Where as this Infant lay,
They found Him in a manger,
  Where oxen feed on hay,
His mother Mary kneeling down,
  Unto the Lord did pray.
              O tidings, &c.

With sudden joy and gladness
  The shepherds were beguiled,
To see the Babe of Israel,
  Before His mother mild.
O then with joy and cheerfulness
  Rejoice, each mother's child.
              O tidings, &c.

Now to the Lord sing praises
  All you within this place,
And with true love and brotherhood
  Each other now embrace,
This holy tide of Christmas
  All others doth deface.
              O tidings, &c.

God bless the ruler of this house
  And send him long to reign,
And many a merry Christmas
  May he live to see again
Among his friends and kindred
  That live both far and near;
  And God send you a happy New Year.

A VIRGIN MOST PURE.

THIS carol has enjoyed great popularity, particularly in the West of England. There are other versions commencing—

"A Virgin unspotted the Prophets did tell
Should bring forth a Saviour, as now it befell," &c.

And—

"A Virgin unspotted, as Prophets foretold
Hath brought forth a young Son, which now we behold," &c.

And there is yet another variation commencing with the burthen " Rejoice and be merry," and otherwise differing from the present. Hone has entered this latter and the version now given in his list as distinct carols. There are certain expressions in the present carol which convey the idea of its possessing some claim to be called ancient. The first of the versions commencing " A Virgin unspotted," was printed by the Rev. Arthur Bedford (the author of several curious works on music and the stage) about the year 1734. Mr. Bedford, in the title of the carol, has given us a singular etymological derivation of the word *carol* from *Carolus*; viz. " A Christmas carol, so called because such were in use in K. Charles I. Reign."! The reader of the present volume will not, it is feared, entertain a very high opinion of Mr. Bedford's antiquarian learning, at least on the subject of Christmas carols.

VIRGIN most pure, as the Prophets did tell,
Hath brought forth a Baby, as it hath befell,
To be our Redeemer from death, hell, and sin,
Which Adam's transgression hath wrapped us in.
Rejoice and be merry, set sorrow aside,
Christ Jesus our Saviour was born on this tide.

RELIGIOUS CAROLS.

In Bethlehem, a city in Jewry it was,—
Where Joseph and Mary together did pass,
And there to be taxed, with many one mo,[1]
For Cæsar commanded the same should be so.
      Rejoice, &c.

But when they had entered the city so fair,
A number of people so mighty was there,
That Joseph and Mary, whose substance was small,
Could get in the city no lodging at all.
      Rejoice, &c.

Then they were constrained in a stable to lie,
Where oxen and asses they used to tie;
Their lodging so simple, they held it no scorn,
But against the next morning our Saviour was born.
      Rejoice, &c.

The King of all Glory to the world being brought,
Small store of fine linen to wrap him was sought;
When Mary had swaddled her young Son so sweet,
In an ox's manger she laid him to sleep.
      Rejoice, &c.

Then God sent an Angel from heaven so high,
To certain poor shepherds in fields where they lie,
And bid them no longer in sorrow to stay,
Because that our Saviour was born on this day.
      Rejoice, &c.

[1] more.

RELIGIOUS CAROLS.

Then presently after, the shepherds did spy
A number of Angels appear in the sky,
Who joyfully talked, and sweetly did sing,
" To God be all Glory, our Heavenly King."
Rejoice, &c.

Three certain Wise Princes they thought it most meet,
To lay their rich offerings at our Saviour's feet;
So then they consented, and to Bethlehem did go,
And when they came thither, they found it was so.
Rejoice, &c.

REMEMBER, O THOU MAN.

THIS " Christmas carol " was printed, in 1611, in the curious musical work of Thomas Ravenscroft, entitled "Melismata. Mvsicall Phansies. Fitting the Covrt, Citie, and Covntrey Hvmovrs. To 3, 4 and 5 Voyces. To all delightfull, except to the Spitefull, To none offensiue, except to the Pensiue." It is there set to music in four parts. In 1665, 1669 and 1682 the carol with its tune only was given in the several editions of a collection of " Song and Fancies, To severall Musicall Parts," which was printed by John Forbes at Aberdeen. Considerable attention was attracted to the latter work some forty years since by an idle assertion that the melody of the well-known song " God, save the king " was derived from that of " Remember, O thou man." A paraphrase of the carol appeared in " Ane compendious Booke of Godly and Spirituall Songs, with sundrie Ballates changed out of prophaine Songes &c," which was printed by Andro Hart in Edinburgh in 1621. It commences—

> Remember, man, remember, man,
> That I thy saull from Sathan wan,
> And has done for thee what I can, &c.

The Elizabethan writers designated carols like the present, " Suffering Ballads."

RELIGIOUS CAROLS.

The carol is now printed from a copy of the *Melismata* in the library of the Sacred Harmonic Society, and collated with a copy of the 1682 edition of Forbes's publication in the same collection. The verse included between brackets does not however appear in either of those copies, but is added from a broadside of later date.

EMEMBER, O thou Man,
  O thou Man, O thou Man,
  Remember, O thou Man,
    Thy time is spent.
Remember, O thou Man,
How thou art dead and gone,
And I did what I can,
    Therefore repent.

Remember Adam's fall,
O thou Man, O thou Man,
Remember Adam's fall
    From Heaven to Hell:
Remember Adam's fall,
How we were condemned all,
In Hell perpetual,
    There for to dwell.

Remember God's goodness,
O thou Man, O thou Man,
Remember God's goodness
    And promise made.
Remember God's goodness,
How he sent his Son, doubtless,
Our sins for to redress,
    Be not afraid.

RELIGIOUS CAROLS.

The Angels all did sing,
O thou Man, O thou Man,
The Angels all did sing
  Upon the Shepherds' hill.
The Angels all did sing
Praises to our Heavenly King,
And peace to man living,
  With a good will.

The shepherds amazed was,
O thou Man, O thou Man,
The shepherds amazed was
  To hear the Angels sing.
The Shepherds amazed was
How this should come to pass,
That Christ our Messias
  Should be our King.

To Bethlehem did they go,
O thou Man, O thou Man,
To Bethlehem did they go,
  The Shepherds three,
To Bethlehem did they go,
To see where it were so or no,
Whether Christ were born or no,
  To set man free.

As the Angels before did say,
O thou Man, O thou Man,
As the Angels before did say,
  So it came to pass.

RELIGIOUS CAROLS.

As the Angels before did say,
They found a babe where as it lay.
In a manger wrapt in hay,
    So poor he was.

In Bethlehem he was born,
O thou Man, O thou Man,
In Bethlehem he was born
    For mankind's sake.
In Bethlehem he was born
For us that were forlorn,
And therefore took no scorn
    Our flesh to take.

[In a manger laid he was,
O thou Man, O thou Man,
In a manger laid he was
    At this time present.
In a manger laid he was
Between an ox and an ass,
And all for our trespass,
    Therefore repent.]

Give thanks to God alway,
O thou Man, O thou Man,
Give thanks to God alway,
    With heart most joyfully:
Give thanks to God alway,
For this our happy day
Let all men sing and say
    Holy, holy.

THE WORCESTERSHIRE CHRISTMAS CAROL.

This Carol possesses a qualification which in the eyes of many entitles it to great consideration;—that of rarity. It has only been met with on two broadsides, both bearing the above title, and both printed at Birmingham at a not very distant date, and in a collection published under the pseudonym of Joshua Sylvester in 1861. To something like an affectation of sonorousness, the author has united a truthfulness of expression which render this one of the most pleasing of modern carols.

OW grand and how bright
 That wonderful night
When angels to Bethlehem came;
 They burst forth like fires,
 They struck their gold lyres,
And mingled their sound with the flame.

 The shepherds were amazed,
 The pretty lambs gazed,
At darkness thus turned into light,
 No voice was there heard,
 From man, beast, or bird,
So sudden and solemn the sight.

 And then when the sound
 Re-echoed around,
The hills and the dales all awoke,
 The moon and the stars
 Stopt their fiery ears,
And listened while Gabriel spoke:—

RELIGIOUS CAROLS.

" I bring yon," said he,
" From the glorious tree,
A message both gladsome and good,
　The Saviour is come
　To the world as His home,
But He lies in a manger of wood."

At mention of this,
The source of all bliss,
The Angels sang loudly and long,
　They soared to the sky,
　Beyond mortal eye,
But left us the words of their song:—

" All glory to God,
Who laid by His rod,
To smile on the world through His Son,
　And peace be on earth,
　For this wonderful birth
Most wonderful conquests has won.

" And good will to man,
Though his life's but a span,
And his soul all sinful and vile."
　Then pray, Christians, pray,
　And let Christmas Day
Have a tear as well as a smile.

A NEW CHRISTMAS CAROL.

This was a favourite in the metropolis in the early part of the present century, and is to be seen on broad sheets then printed in Bloomsbury and Clerkenwell. It has only once, however, been reprinted in a collection.

T is the day, the Holy day,
   On which our Lord was born,
   And sweetly do the sunbeams gild
     The dew besprinkled thorn.
The birds sing thro' the heavens,
   And the breezes gently play,
And song and sunshine lovely,
   Begin this Holy day.

'Twas in a humble manger,
   A little lowly shed,
With cattle at His infant feet,
   And shepherds at His head,
The Saviour of this sinful world,
   In innocence first lay,
While Wise Men made their offerings
   To Him this Holy day.

He comes to save the perishing,
   To waft the sighs to heaven
Of guilty men, who truly sought
   To weep, to be forgiven.

RELIGIOUS CAROLS.

An Intercessor still He shines,
    And men to Him should pray,
At His altar's feet, for meekness
    Upon this Holy day.

As flowers still bloom fair again,
    Though all their life seems shed,
Thus we shall rise with life once more,
    Tho' number'd with the dead.
Then may our stations be near Him,
    To whom we worship pay,
And praise with heart-felt gratitude,
    Upon this Holy day.

A CAROL FOR ST. STEPHEN'S DAY.

This carol is contained in a manuscript in the British Museum of the period of Henry VI. Dr. Prior, in his excellent collection of Ancient Danish Ballads, has given a Danish version, in which Stephen is represented not as a clerk or sewer, but a stable boy. Of the legend, which is of much older date than the carol, Dr. Prior thus speaks: " The story of the cock was originally applied to other Saints, as St. James, St. Peter, or the Virgin. The oldest account of it is in Vinc. Bellovacensis, from an author who lived about 1200. Two friends sat down to dinner in Bologna, and one bade the other to carve the cock, which he did, so that, as he said, not St. Peter or our Lord Himself could put it together again. The cock sprang up, clapped his wings and crowed, scattering the sauce over the two friends, and rendering them lepers until the day of their death. The same miracle is related as having occurred to prove the innocence of persons falsely accused, and is found in the legends of Spain, Brittany, Italy, and Sclavonian countries. How it came to be appropriated to St. Stephen does not appear." The odd anachronism of making the martyrdom of Stephen occur under Herod will not escape the reader's observation.

AINT Stephen was a clerk
In king Herod his hall,
And served him of bread and cloth
As ever king befall.[1]

Stephen out of kitchen came
With boar his head on hand,
He saw a star was fair and bright
Over Bethlem stand.

[1] happened to.

RELIGIOUS CAROLS.

He cast adown the boar his head,
    And went into the hall;
" I forsake thee, king Herod,
    And thy works all.

" I forsake thee, king Herod,
    And thy works all,
There is a child in Bethlem born,
    Is better than we all."

" What aileth thee, Stephen,
    What is thee befall?
Lacketh thee either meat or drink,
    In king Herod his hall?"

" Lacketh me neither meat nor drink
    In king Herod his hall,
There is a child in Bethlem born,
    Is better than we all."

" What aileth thee, Stephen,
    Art thou wode,[1] or thou ginnest to brede?[2]
Lacketh thee either gold or fee,
    Or any rich weed?"[3]

" Lacketh me neither gold nor fee,
    Nor none rich weed,
There is a child in Bethlem bore
    Shall help us at our need."

[1] mad.   [2] upbraid.   [3] dress.

RELIGIOUS CAROLS.

"That is all so sooth, Stephen,
    All so sooth, I wis,
As this capon crow shall,
    That lyeth here in my dish."

That word was not so soon said,
    That word in that hall,
The capon crew, *Christus natus est!*
    Among the lords all.

Riseth up my tormentors,[1]
    By two, and all by one,
And leadeth Stephen out of this town,
    And stoneth him with stone.

Tooken they Stephen,
    And stoned him in the way,
And therefore is his even,
    On Christ his own day.

[1] executioners.

A CAROL FOR ST. STEPHEN'S DAY.

THIS is a north-country carol and is principally to be met with in the broad-sheets printed at Newcastle during the last and present centuries. An abbreviated version, with some alterations, which are anything but improvements, is given in some of the broadsides issued from the Seven-Dials press of the well-known Catnach. It has not been given in any preceding collection of carols.

N friendly love and unity
    For good St. Stephen's sake,
    Let us all this blessed day
        To heaven our prayers make;
That we with him the Cross of Christ
    May freely undertake,
        And Jesus will send you His blessing.

Those accursed infidels
    That stoned him to death,
Could not by their cruelties
    Withhold him from his faith:
In such a godly martyrdom,
    Seek we all the path,
        And Jesus will send you His blessing.

RELIGIOUS CAROLS.

And whilst we sit here banquetting,
   Of dainties having store,
Let us not forgetful be
   To cherish up the poor,
And give what is convenient
   To those that ask at door.
      And Jesus will send you His blessing.

For God has made you stewards here
   Upon the earth to dwell;
He that gathereth for himself,
   And will not use it well,
Lives far worse than devils do
   That burneth now in hell.
      And Jesus will send you His blessing.

And now in love and charity
   See you your table spread;
That I may taste of your good cheer,
   Your Christmas ale and bread,
That I may say that I full well
   For this my carol sped.
      And Jesus will send you His blessing.

For bounty is a blessed gift,
   The Lord above it sends;
And he that gives it from his hands
   Deserveth many friends;
I see it on my master's board;
   And so my carol ends.
      Lord Jesus now send you His blessing.

A CAROL OF THE INNOCENTS.

This Carol was printed in a volume bearing the title of ¶ Christmas carolles newely Inprinted. [Woodcut of Our Saviour crucified between the two thieves.] ¶ Imprinted at London in the Powltry, by Richard Kele, dwelling at the longe shop under saynt Myldredes Chyrche," which was probably published between the years 1546 and 1552, during which time Kele lived at the Long shop in the Poultry, and at the sign of the Eagle near unto Stocks Market in Lombard Street. Seven of the carols contained in Kele's publication were included by the late Dr. Bliss in a small volume of *Bibliographical Miscellanies* which he printed in 1813, and from this volume, (which is now very scarce, the impression having been limited to 104 copies,) the present copy is taken.

The circumstance of Herod's own child being slain in the massacre was believed for centuries. How or when the tradition arose is uncertain, but the circumstance is mentioned by Macrobius, who wrote in the fifth century, in connection with a witticism of the Emperor Augustus Cæsar, who, on hearing the report, said, it was better to be Herod's pig than his son; in allusion to Herod's position as King of the Jews. In " The Slaughter of the Innocents," one of the mysteries formerly performed by the trades of Chester at Whitsuntide, one of Herod's soldiers kills a child in the arms of a woman, who tells him it is the king's son, who had been placed at nurse with her. She rushes to Herod and acquaints him of the murder, on hearing of which he rages, becomes mad, and dies; and a demon comes and carries him into the place of torment.

ARK this song, for it is true,
For it is true as clerks tell:
In old time strange things came to pass,
Great wonder and great marvel was
    In Israel.

RELIGIOUS CAROLS.

There was one Octavian,
Octavian of Rome Emperor,
As books old doth specify,
Of all the wide world truly
    He was lord and governor.

The Jews that time lacked a king,
They lacked a king to guide them well,
The Emperor of power and might,
Chose one Herod against all right,
    In Israel.

This Herod then was King of Jews,
Was King of Jews, and he no Jew,
Forsooth he was a Paynim born,
Wherefore on faith it may be sworn
    He reigned King untrue.

By prophecy one Isai,
One Isai at least did tell
A child should come, wondrous news,
That should be born true King of Jews
    In Israel.

This Herod knew one born should be,
One born should be of true lineage,
That should be right heritor;
For he but by the Emperor
    Was made by usurpage.

RELIGIOUS CAROLS.

Wherefore of thought this King Herod,
This King Herod in great fear fell,
For all the days most in his mirth,
Ever he feared Christ his birth
  In Israel.

The time came it pleased God,
It pleased God so to come to pass,
For man's soul indeed
His blessed Son was born with speed
  As his will was.

Tidings came to King Herod,
To King Herod, and did him tell,
That one born forsooth is he,
Which lord and king of all shall be
  In Israel.

Herod then raged as he were wode,[1]
As he were wode of this tiding,
And sent for all his scribes sure,
Yet would he not trust the Scripture,
  Nor of their counselling.

Then this was the conclusion,
The conclusion of his counsel,
To send unto his knights anon
To slay the children every one
  In Israel.

[1] mad.

RELIGIOUS CAROLS.

This cruel king this tyranny,
This tyranny did put in ure,[1]
Between a day and years two
All men-children he did slew,
  Of Christ for to be sure.

Yet Herod missed his cruel prey,
His cruel prey as was God's will;
Joseph with Mary then did flee
With Christ to Egypt gone was she
  From Israel.

All the while these tyrants,
These tyrants would not convert,
But innocents young
That lay sucking,
  They thrust to the heart.

This Herod sought the children young,
The children young, with courage fell,
But in doing this vengeance
His own son was slain by chance
  In Israel.

Alas! I think the mothers were woe,
The mothers were woe, it was great skill,
What motherly pain
To see them slain
  In cradles lying still!

[1] practice.

RELIGIOUS CAROLS.

But God Himself hath them elect,
Hath them elect, in heaven to dwell,
For they were bathed in their blood,
For their Baptism forsooth it stood
    In Israel.

Alas! again what hearts had they,
What hearts had they those babes to kill,
With swords when they them caught,
In cradles they lay and laughed,
    And never thought ill.

A LULLABY CAROL.

THIS Carol is taken from a scarce and curious musical work entitled, "Psalmes, Sonets and songs of sadnes and pietie, made into Musicke of fiue parts: whereof, some of them going abroad among diuers, in vntrue coppies, are heere truely corrected, and th' other being Songs very rare and newly composed, are heere published, for the recreation of all such as delight in Musicke: By William Byrd one of the Gent: of the Queenes Maiesties Royall Chappell;" which was printed at London, at first without date, in the year 1587, and afterwards with the date of 1588. The work has a dedication to Sir Christopher Hatton, Lord Chancellor of England, the favourite of Elizabeth, known as the "dancing Chancellor,"—

    " Full oft within the spacious walls,
      When he had fifty winters o'er him,
    My grave Lord Keeper led the braules:
      The seal and maces danc'd before him."—

RELIGIOUS CAROLS.

And on the back of the title are some reasons for learning to sing, so excellent and so quaintly expressed, that the reader will not regret their introduction here.

"¶ Reasons briefely set downe by th' author, to perswade euery one to learne to sing.

First, it is a knowledge easely taught, and quickly learned, where there is a good Master, and an apt Scholler.

2. The exercise of singing is delightfull to Nature, and good to preserue the health of Man.

3. It doth strengthen all parts of the brest, and doth open the pipes.

4. It is a singular good remedie for a stutting and stamering in the speech.

5. It is the best meanes to procure a perfect pronounciation, and to make a good Orator.

6. It is the onely way to know where Nature hath bestowed the benefit of a good voyce: which guift is so rare, as there is not one among a thousand, that hath it: and in many, that excellent guift is lost because they want art to expresse Nature.

7. There is not any Musicke of Instruments whatsoeuer, comparable to that which is made of the voyces of Men, where the voyces are good, and the same well sorted and ordered.

8. The better the voyce is, the meeter it is to honour and serue God there-with: and the voyce of man is chiefely to bee imployed to that ende.

Omnis spiritus Laudes Dominum.
Since singing is so good a thing,
I wish all men would learne to sing."

The carol was reprinted by Sir Egerton Brydges in his *Censura Literaria*, and has been thence copied into several collections of carols, but all these copies have defects occasioned by Sir Egerton having used the Tenor part only of Byrd's work. The present copy is given from a complete set of the original part books (the undated edition) now in the library of the Sacred Harmonic Society.

RELIGIOUS CAROLS.

ULLA, la lulla, lulla lullaby,
    My sweet little baby, what meanest thou to cry?
    Be still, my blessed babe, though cause thou hast
        to mourn,
Whose blood most innocent to shed the cruel king hath sworn:
And lo, alas, behold what slaughter he doth make,
Shedding the blood of infants all, sweet Saviour, for Thy sake,
A King is born, they say, which King this king would kill;
Oh wo, and woful heavy day, when wretches have their will.

    Lulla, la lulla, lulla lullaby,
My sweet little baby, what meanest thou to cry?
Three kings this King of kings to see, are come from far,
To each unknown, with offerings great, by guiding of a star!
And shepherds heard the song, which Angels bright did sing,
Giving all glory unto God, for coming of this King,
Which must be made away, King Herod would Him kill;
Oh wo, and woful heavy day, when wretches have their will.

    Lulla, la lulla, lulla lullaby,
My sweet little baby, what meanest thou to cry?
Lo, my little babe, be still, lament no more,
From fury shall thou step aside, help have we still in store;
We heavenly warning have, some other soil to seek,
From death must fly the Lord of life, as Lamb both mild and
    meek:
Thus must my babe obey the king that would him kill,
Oh wo, and woful heavy day, when wretches have their will.

RELIGIOUS CAROLS.

Lulla, la lulla, lulla lullaby,
My sweet little baby, what meanest thou to cry?
But thou shalt live and reign, as Sybils have foresaid,
As all the Prophets prophesy, whose mother, yet a maid,
And perfect Virgin pure, with her breasts shall up-breed
Both God and man that all hath made, the Son of heavenly seed;
Whom caitiffs none can 'tray, whom tyrants none can kill,
Oh joy, and joyful happy day, when wretches want their will.

A BABE IS BORN.

This Carol is of the time of Henry VI. The Latin words with which each verse is terminated are the first lines of hymns used in the church service. This mode of writing was very prevalent amongst the mediæval carolists.

Nowel el el el, now is well
That ever was woe.

BABE is born all of a may,[1]
In the salvation of us,
To them we sing both night and day,
Veni Creator Spiritus.

At Bethlehem that blessed place,
The child of bliss born He was,
Him to serve God give us grace,
O Lux Beata Trinitas.

[1] maid.

RELIGIOUS CAROLS.

There came three kings out of the east,
    To worship the King that is so free,
With gold and myrrh and frankincense,
    A solis ortus cardine.

The herds heard an Angel cry,
    A merry song then sung he,
Why are ye so sore aghast?
    Jam ortus solis cardine.

The Angel came down with a cry,
    A fair song then sung he,
In the worship of that child,
    Gloria Tibi, Domine.

WHEN CHRIST WAS BORN.

This Carol (which is of the same description as the last) is preserved in a manuscript written early in the sixteenth century, and now in the British Museum.

Christo paremus canticam, Excelsis Gloria.

HEN Christ was born of Mary free,
    In Bethlehem in that fair city,
Angels sang with mirth and glee,
    In Excelsis Gloria!

RELIGIOUS CAROLS.

Herdsmen beheld the Angels bright,
To them appeared with great light,
And said, " God's Son is born this night,"
In Excelsis Gloria!

This King is come to save mankind,
As in Scripture we do find,
Therefore this song have we in mind,
In Excelsis Gloria!

Then, Lord, for Thy great Grace,
Grant us the bliss to see Thy face,
Where we may sing to Thy solace,
In Excelsis Gloria!

BE WE MERRY IN THIS FEAST.

THIS is a carol of the same kind as the preceding. It was originally printed by Richard Kele in the small volume mentioned in the note on the Carol of the Innocents.

Be we merry in this feast,
In quo Salvator natus est.

N Bethlehem, that noble place,
As by prophecy said it was,
Of the Virgin Mary, full of grace,
Salvator mundi natus est.
        Be we merry, &c.

RELIGIOUS CAROLS.

On Christmas night an Angel it told
To the shepherds keeping their fold
That in Bethlehem with beasts wolde,[1]
Salvator mundi natus est.
    Be we merry, &c.

The shepherds were compassed right,
About them was a great light,
" Dread ye naught," said the Angel bright,
" *Salvator mundi natus est.*"
    Be we merry, &c.

" Behold! to you we bring great joy.
For why? Jesus is born to-day
Of Mary, that mild may.[2]
Salvator mundi natus est."
    Be we merry, &c.

" And thus in faith find it ye shall,
Lying poorly in an ox's stall."
The shepherds then lauded God all,
Quia Salvator mundi natus est.
    Be we merry in this feast,
    Salvator mundi natus est.

[1] wild (?). [2] maid.

THE JOYFUL SOUNDS OF SALVATION.

This was formerly a favourite Carol in the metropolis, as the numerous copies emanating from the Seven-Dials and Smithfield presses prove, but does not seem to have been reprinted of late years. Some of its verses are almost identical with those of the carol " A Virgin most pure." It is now first included in a collection of carols.

N the reign of great Cæsar, the emp'ror of Rome,
The first work of salvation for sinners was done
By Heaven's decree,—for a Babe then was sent
As a ransom for sinners—so let us repent.

Great Cæsar commanded and ordered it so,
~~All~~ The world should be taxed, the high and the low ;
Each ~~Every~~ one to his city this tax went to pay,
So strict was this despot in absolute sway.

~~Then~~ From Naz'reth to Bethlem in Jewry it was,
That Joseph and Mary together did pass ;
These two to be taxèd with others did go,
For Cæsar commanded and ordered it so.

They both having entered the city so fair,
Such numbers of people so mighty were there,
That Joseph and Mary, their substance being small,
Could get at the inns no lodging at all.

RELIGIOUS CAROLS.

So they were constrain'd in a stable to lie,
Where oxen and asses they used to tie;
Although mean their lodging they thought it no scorn;
And early next morning our Saviour was born.

Then God sent an Angel from heaven so high
To certain poor shepherds in fields that did lie,
And bade them no longer in sorrow to stay,
For their blessed Saviour was born on that day.

And presently after the shepherds did spy
A great number of Angels appear in the sky, [host]
Who merrily talkèd, and sweetly did sing;
All glory to God and their heavenly King.

He's the Prince of Salvation, so be not afraid;
With this salutation to the shepherds they said,
Be ye no longer strangers, for in swaddling clothes
The Babe lies in a manger. So the shepherds arose,

Being resolved together to Bethlehem to go;
And when they came thither they found it was so.
So let us be merry in a moderate way,
Sing praises with homage, and honour the day.

The great King of Glory to this world being brought,
God's love for poor sinners with wonder was wrought:
And when they had swaddled our Saviour so sweet,
In an ox's manger they laid him to sleep.

RELIGIOUS CAROLS.

At Bethlehem in Judea the slaughter begun
By king Herod's orders; to make sure of one,
Many thousands of smiling young infants were slain;
To murder our Saviour was the tyrant's aim.

Then Joseph, being warned by God in a dream,
He arose and took Jesus and Mary with him,
And fled for a season into Egypt, where
The Child and its Mother preserved were there.

God's love to the world, lost sinners to free,
His love's so enduring to both thee and me:
So let us love each other, to no hatred inclined;
For Christ died to save all the race of mankind.

THE CHERRY-TREE CAROL.

THIS carol has long been a favourite with the people, and is met with on broadsides printed in all parts of England. The legend of the cherry-tree is very ancient. The fifteenth of the mysteries represented at Coventry on the feast of Corpus Christi in the fifteenth century, if not earlier, is entitled "The Birth of Christ," and the opening scene represents Joseph and Mary on their way to Bethlehem. Mary, perceiving a cherry-tree, requests her husband to pluck her some of the fruit for which she has a longing. Joseph rudely refuses in much the same terms as in the carol. Mary prays God to grant her the boon to have of the cherries, and the tree immediately bows down to her. Joseph, seeing this, repents of his jealousy and unkindness, and asks forgiveness. There are many

RELIGIOUS CAROLS.

versions of this carol, some with omissions, others with additions, but that now given seemed the most preferable. The latter portion, commencing at the verse "As Joseph was a walking," is sometimes given as a separate carol under the title of "Joseph and the Angel." Joseph's advanced age is mentioned in many places in the Apocryphal New Testament; as in the Gospel of the birth of Mary, where he is called "a person very far advanced in years," and in the Protevangelion, where he is represented as saying, "I am an old man." Hone, who gives a version of this carol, says, "The admiration of my earliest days, for some lines in the Cherry carol still remains, nor can I help thinking that the reader will see somewhat of cause for it."

OSEPH was an old man,
    And an old man was he,
  And he married Mary
    The Queen of Galilee.

When Joseph was married
    And Mary home had brought,
Mary proved with child
    And Joseph knew it not.

Joseph and Mary walked
    Through a garden gay,
Where the cherries they grew
    Upon every tree.

O then bespoke Mary,
    With words both meek and mild,
" O gather me cherries, Joseph,
    They run so in my mind."

RELIGIOUS CAROLS.

And then replied Joseph
  With his words so unkind,
" Let him gather thee cherries
  That got thee with child."

O then bespoke our Saviour,
  All in His mother's womb,
" Bow down, good cherry-tree,
  To my mother's hand."

The uppermost sprig
  Bowed down to Mary's knee,
" Thus you may see, Joseph,
  These cherries are for me."

" O eat your cherries, Mary,
  O eat your cherries now,
O eat your cherries, Mary,
  That grow upon the bough."

As Joseph was a walking
  He heard an Angel sing :—
" This night shall be born
  Our Heavenly King ;

" He neither shall be born
  In housen, nor in hall,
Nor in the place of Paradise,
  But in an ox's stall ;

RELIGIOUS CAROLS.

"He neither shall be clothed
 In purple nor in pall,
But all in fair linen,
 As were babies all;

"He neither shall be rocked
 In silver nor in gold,
But in a wooden cradle,
 That rocks on the mould;

"He neither shall be christened
 In white wine nor red,
But with fair spring water
 With which we were christened."

Then Mary took her young Son,
 And set him on her knee:—
"I pray thee now, dear child,
 Tell how this world shall be?"

"O, I shall be as dead, Mother,
 As the stones in the wall;
O, the stones in the street, Mother,
 Shall mourn for me all.

"And upon a Wednesday
 My vow I will make,
And upon Good Friday
 My death I will take;

RELIGIOUS CAROLS.

"Upon Easter-day, Mother,
  My rising shall be;
O, the sun and the moon,
  Shall uprise with me."

The people shall rejoice,
  And the birds they shall sing
To see the uprising
  Of the Heavenly King.

THE MOON SHONE BRIGHT.

THIS carol is much in use in the midland and western counties. A shorter version is found on sheets issued by the Seven Dials printers, and likewise on west-country broadsides (on which the present version also appears), under the title of "The Bellman." In the Seven Dials copy the fourth line runs, "And hark! the bellman of the night." Both versions have much the appearance of being what were formerly called, "Bellman's Verses." The functionary known in bygone times as the Bellman was a kind of night watchman, who, in addition to his staff and lantern, carried a bell, and at a certain period of the year was wont to arouse the slumbering inhabitants of the town to listen to some such effusion as that now printed. For this service (?) he looked for some gratuity at Christmas. Herrick has a little poem called "The Bellman," which takes the form of these nocturnal addresses:—

"From noise of scare-fires rest ye free,
From murders Benedicite;
From all mischances that may fright
Your pleasing slumbers in the night
Mercy secure ye all, and keep
The goblin from ye while ye sleep.
Past one o'clock, and almost two;
My masters all, Good day to you."

RELIGIOUS CAROLS.

And we must not forget Milton's mention in his "Il Penseroso," of

"the belman's drowsy charm
To bless the doors from nightly harm."

In a scarce and curious tract, first published in 1608, by Thomas Dekker, the dramatist and satirist, under the title of "The Belman of London, bringing to light the most notorious villanies that are now practised in the kingdome," there is a woodcut engraving representing a Bellman of the period going his rounds, who carries a staff, lantern, and bell, and is followed by his dog.

One of the verses of Shakespeare's song, "It was a lover and his lass" (sung by the two pages in "As you like it"), runs thus:—

"This *Carroll* they began that houre
With a hey, and a ho, and a hey nonino;
How that a life was but a flower
In spring time," &c.

which may possibly allude to the present carol, or to some other containing a passage similar to the sixth verse of this.

Several lines of this carol are incorporated into a Mayers' Song, sung in Hertfordshire, a copy of which is given in Hone's "Every-day Book," vol. i. col. 567, and some lines are also found in another version of the same song, which continues in use in Huntingdonshire, a copy of which may be seen in "Notes and Queries," 3rd series, ix. 388.

HE moon shone bright
  And the stars gave a light
A little before it was day.
The Lord our God he call'd on us
And bade us awake and pray.

Awake, awake, good people all,
 Awake and you shall hear,
The Lord our God died on the cross,
 For us whom He loved so dear.

RELIGIOUS CAROLS.

O fair, O fair Jerusalem,
    When shall we come to thee?
When shall our sorrows have an end,
    Thy joy that we may see?

The fields were green as green could be,
    When from His glorious seat
Our blessed Father watered us,
    With His heavenly dew so sweet.

And for the saving of our souls
    Christ died upon the Cross;
We ne'er shall do for Jesus Christ
    As He has done for us.

The life of man is but a span,
    And cut down in its flower,
We are here to-day, to-morrow gone,
    The creatures of an hour.

Instruct and teach your children well,
    The while that you are here;
It will be better for your soul
    When your corpse lies on the bier.

To-day you may be alive and well,
    Worth many a thousand pound,
To-morrow dead and cold as clay,
    Your corpse laid under ground.

RELIGIOUS CAROLS.

With one turf at your head, O man,
 And another at your feet,
Thy good deeds and thy bad, O man,
 Will altogether meet.

My song is done, I must begone,
 I can stay no longer here,
God bless you all, both great and small,
 And send you a joyful new year!

COME REJOICE, ALL GOOD CHRISTIANS.

THIS carol is believed to be of some antiquity. It is still reprinted in the broadsides issued at Christmas. The burden is nearly the same, it will be observed, as that of the West-country carol, "A Virgin most pure," and possibly the present carol had its birth in the same part of the country.

OME rejoice, all good Christians,
 And rejoice now, I pray,
For joy our Redeemer
 Was born on this day,
In the city of David,
 At a cottage so poor:
Then rejoice and be you merry,
 We have blessings in store.
  And therefore be you merry,
  Rejoice and be you merry,
  Set sorrows away,
  Christ Jesus, our Saviour,
  Was born on this day.

RELIGIOUS CAROLS.

Our Lord He was born
  Of a Virgin most pure,
Within a poor stable
  Both safe and secure;
He was guarded most safely
  With Angels so bright,
Who told three poor Shepherds
  Those things in the night.
      And therefore, &c.

They said, " Be not fearful,
  But to Bethlehem go;
Then rejoice and be cheerful
  For 'tis certainly so:
For a young son to Joseph
  Is in Bethlehem born,
Then rejoice, all good Christians,
  And cease for to mourn."
      And therefore, &c.

And when those three Shepherds
  Did to Bethlehem come,
And arrived at the stable,
  Then in they did run.
Where they found blessed Mary
  With Jesus her Son;
There they found our Lord sleeping,
  And thus they begun.
      And therefore, &c.

RELIGIOUS CAROLS.

With the sweetest Hallelujah
　　The Heavens did rejoice,
With the Saints and the Angels,
　　And all with sweet voice,
Crying, " Glory and honour
　　To our Heavenly king!"
In the clouds of the air
　　Then this Host they did sing.
　　　　　And therefore, &c.

Then well may we Christians,
　　That dwell on the earth,
Rejoice and be glad
　　For sweet Jesus his birth,
Who brought us salvation,
　　If we mind but the same:
Then let all in the nation
　　Sing praise to His Name.
　　　　　And therefore, &c.

With true zeal and honour
　　Let us joyfully sing,
In praise of our salvation,
　　To our Heavenly King:
To our Heavenly Father,
　　That remaineth above,
And to our dear Saviour,
　　That redeem'd us with love.
　　　　　And therefore, &c.

THE ANGEL GABRIEL.

THIS carol is much used in the Western counties, and it is to its popularity, rather than its literary merit, that it is indebted for its place in this collection. The line in the second stanza, "As the lot fell unto me," alludes to the manner in which Joseph was miraculously pointed out as the husband of the Virgin by a flower budding forth from his rod and the Holy Ghost, in the form of a dove, descending thereon, as related in the Apocryphal Gospel of the Birth of Mary. This circumstance is introduced into the tenth of the Coventry Mysteries, "Mary's Betrothment."

HE Angel Gabriel from God
    Was sent to Galilee,
Unto a Virgin fair and free,
    Whose name was called Mary.
And when the Angel thither came,
    He fell down on his knee,
And looking up in the Virgin's face,
    He said, "All hail, Mary!"
        Then, sing we all, both great and small,
            Noël, Noël, Noël;
        We may rejoice to hear the voice
            Of the Angel Gabriel.

Mary anon looked him upon,
    And said, "Sir, what are ye?

RELIGIOUS CAROLS.

I marvel much at these tidings
    Which thou hast brought to me.
Married I am unto an old man,
    As the lot fell unto me;
Therefore I pray depart away,
    For I stand in doubt of thee."
          Then, sing, &c.

"Mary," he said, "be not afraid,
    But do believe in me:
The power of the Holy Ghost
    Shall overshadow thee;
Thou shalt conceive without any grief,
    As the Lord told unto me;
God's own dear Son from Heaven shall come,
    And shall be born of thee."
          Then, sing, &c.

This came to pass as God's will was,
    Even as the Angel told.
About midnight an Angel bright
    Came to the Shepherds' fold,
And told them then both where and when
    Born was the child, our Lord,
And all along this was their song,
    "All glory be given to God."
          Then, sing, &c.

Good people all, both great and small,
    The which do hear my voice,

RELIGIOUS CAROLS.

With one accord let's praise the Lord,
    And in our hearts rejoice ;
Like sister and brother, let's love one another
    Whilst we our lives do spend,
Whilst we have space let's pray for grace,
    And so let my Carol end.
              Then, sing, &c.

THE BABE OF BETHLEHEM.

THIS is a carol which has attained a considerable degree of popularity; yet it is, notwithstanding, one of the feeblest and poorest so distinguished. It is one of those productions which finds favour with the managers of the (so-called) religious societies, who include it in their collections and on their sheets, a circumstance to be lamented, as they might surely find better productions than this for dissemination. But for its long-continued popularity it would not have been accorded a place in this collection. The versions of the societies have a kind of varying refrain, which is not found in the copy whence the present is taken, and which it has not been thought necessary to reproduce here.

COME, behold the Virgin Mother,
    Fondly leaning on her child,
    Nature shows not such another,
    Glorious, holy, meek and miild :
Bethlehem's ancient walls inclose Him,
    Dwelling place of David once ;
Now no friendly homestead knows Him,
    Tho' the noblest of his sons.

RELIGIOUS CAROLS.

Many a prophecy before Him
    Published His bright advent long,
Guardian Angels low adore Him
    In a joyous heavenly song;
Eastern Sages see with wonder
    His bright star illume the sky,
O'er the volumes old they ponder,
    Volumes of dark prophecy.

Royal Bethlehem how deserted,
    All its pomp and splendour lost;
Is a stable, vile and dirty,
    All the welcome you can boast?
Far they travel, oft inquiring
    Where the wondrous Babe is born:
On they come with great desiring,
    Although others treat with scorn.

See, a Babe of days and weakness
    Heaven's Almighty now appears,
Liable to death and sickness,
    Shame and agony and tears.
Sovereign He, and great Creator,
    He who form'd the heav'ns and earth
Yet takes on Him human nature,
    Angels wonder at His birth.

Why, ah, why this condescension,
    God with mortal man to dwell?

RELIGIOUS CAROLS.

Why lay by His grand pretension,
   He who does all thrones excel?
'Tis to be a man, a brother,
   With us sinners of mankind:
Vain we search for such another,
   Ne'er we love like this shall find.

'Tis to make Himself an offering
   As a pure atoning lamb,
Souls redeeming by His suffering,
   That in human flesh He came;
As a God He could not suffer,
   He a body true must have;
As a man what He might offer
   Could not satisfy or save.

Tho' an infant now you view Him,
   He shall fill His Father's throne,
Gather all the Nations to Him;
   Every knee shall then bow down:
Foes shall at His presence tremble,
   Great and small, and quick and dead,
None can fly, none dare dissemble,
   None find where to hide his head.

Friends! Oh then in cheerful voices
   They shall shout with glad acclaim,
While each rising saint rejoices,
   Saints of high or lowest fame.

RELIGIOUS CAROLS.

Then what different appearing
　　We 'mong mortal tribes shall find;
Groaning those who now are sneering,
　　Triumphing the humble mind.

May we now, that day forestalling,
　　Hear the word, and read and pray,
Listen to the Gospel calling,
　　And with humble heart obey.
Give us hearty true repentance,
　　Live in faith and holiness;
Then we need not fear Thy sentence,
　　But may trust Thy saving grace,
　　　　　　Hallelujah, Hallelujah, Hallelujah,
　　　　　　　　Praise the Lord.

JOY TO THE WORLD.

THIS is a carol which is greatly admired in Devonshire and Cornwall, and obtains a place in many a collection of sheet carols printed in the West. It is certainly a hundred and fifty years of age, and may be even older. The first two lines are identical with those of a hymn by Isaac Watts, produced about 1709, of which the third and fourth lines are—

　　"Let every heart prepare Him room,
　　　'And heaven and nature sing;"

RELIGIOUS CAROLS.

but the remainder is entirely different. Perhaps the popularity of Watts's verses may have tempted the carolist to commit a little plagiarism.

JOY to the world, the Lord is come,
    Let earth receive her King;
Let every tongue with sacred mirth
    His loud applauses sing.

Hark, hark, what news, what joyful news,
    To all the nations round;
To-day rejoice, a King is born,
    Who is with glory crown'd.

Behold! He comes, the tidings spread,
    A Saviour full of grace:
He comes, in mercy, to restore
    A sinful, fallen race.

HARK! ALL AROUND THE WELKIN RINGS.

This is a West of England carol. It was included by Davies Gilbert in the second edition of his collection of Ancient Christmas Carols (1823), and is still to be found on the common broadsides.

HARK! all around the welkin rings,
    Bright seraphs hail the morn
That ushers in the King of Kings,
    That sees a Saviour born.

RELIGIOUS CAROLS.

Chorus.
Ye people on earth, your voices now raise,
To Christ our Redeemer, in carols of praise,
Hallelujah! praise the Lord, Hallelujah!

The shining heralds from on high
  These joyful tidings bear
With acclamations down the sky,
  And humble shepherds hear.

"Glory to God, and peace to men,"
  The heavenly choir did sing;
Let earth repeat the sound again,
  And hail the new-born King.

This is the day our Lord did choose
  To visit mortal man;
And from the bands of sin to loose
  All those that trust in Him.

Lord Jesus, let Thy kingdom spread
  Through all the earth below;
Let every land Thy wonders read,
  And Thy salvation know.

Hosanna! let all earth and heaven
  Salute the happy morn;
To-day the promis'd Child is given,
  And God Himself is born.

MORTALS, AWAKE, WITH ANGELS JOIN.

This is found on the West-country broadsides with sufficient frequency to indicate a large share of popularity. It seems a comparatively modern production, and probably owes its birth to some of the hymn-writers of the last century. The broadside printers place the fifth verse between brackets, possibly to indicate its being an addition to the original carol.

ORTALS, awake, with Angels join,
    And chant the solemn lay;
Joy, love, and gratitude combine
    To hail the auspicious day.

In Heaven the rapturous song began,
    And sweet seraphic fire
Through all the shining legions ran,
    And strung and tun'd the lyre.

Swift through the vast expanse it flew,
    And loud the echo roll'd;
The theme, the song, the joy was new,
    'Twas more than heaven could hold.

Down thro' the portals of the sky
    Th' impetuous torrent ran;
And Angels flew with eager joy
    To bear the news to man.

RELIGIOUS CAROLS.

[Wrapt in the silence of the night
    Lay all the eastern world,
When bursting, glorious, heavenly light
    The wondrous scene unfurl'd.]

Hark! the Cherubic armies shout,
    And glory leads the song;
Good will and peace are heard throughout
    Th' harmonious heavenly throng.

O for a glance of heavenly love
    Our hearts and songs to raise,
Sweetly to bear our souls above,
    And mingle with their lays!

With joy the chorus we'll repeat,
    " Glory to God on high!
Good-will and peace are now complete;
    Jesus was born to die."

Hail, Prince of Life! for ever hail!
    Redeemer, brother, friend!
Tho' earth, and time, and life should fail,
    Thy praise shall never end.

A CAROL FOR NEW-YEAR'S DAY.

This carol is contained, under the above title, in the scarce musical work called "Psalmes, Songs, and Sonnets: Some solemne, others ioyfull, framed to the life of the Words; Fit for Voyces or Viols of 3, 4, 5, and 6 parts. Composed by William Byrd, one of the Gent. of his Maiesties honourable Chappell." London, 1611. It is now given from a copy of that work in the library of the Sacred Harmonic Society, and is believed never to have been included in any previous collection of carols.

GOD, that guides the cheerful sun
    By motions strange the year to frame,
Which now, returned whence it begun,
    From heaven extols Thy glorious Name,
This New-year's season sanctify,
    With double blessings of Thy store,
That graces new may multiply,
    And former follies reign no more.
So shall our hearts with heaven agree,
And both give laud and praise to Thee.   Amen.

Th' old year by course is past and gone,
    Old Adam, Lord, from us expel:
New creatures make us every one,
    New life becomes the New year well.
As new born babes from malice keep,
    New wedding garments, O Christ, we crave;

RELIGIOUS CAROLS.

That we Thy face in heaven may see
  With Angels bright our souls to save.
So shall our hearts with heaven agree,
And both give laud and praise to Thee.   Amen.

THE THREE KINGS.

A CAROL FOR THE EPIPHANY.

THIS carol is found in a manuscript of the time of Henry VII, now amongst the Harleian manuscripts in the British Museum. Another manuscript in the same collection contains the legend of the Three Kings; and from this we learn that they were Melchior, King of Nubia and Arabia, who offered to the Saviour gold, and who is described as the least of stature and of person; Baltazar, King of Godoly and of Saba, who offered incense, and was of mean stature in his person; and Jasper, who was King of Taars (or Tharsis) and of (the isle of) Egripwille, who offered myrrh, and was "most in person, and was a black Ethiop." Thus was fulfilled the Psalmist's prophecy, "The Kings of Tharsis and of the Isles shall bring presents; the Kings of Arabia and Saba shall bring gifts." They were afterwards baptized by St. Thomas the Apostle, and long after their deaths, their bodies were conveyed by the Empress Helena, the mother of Constantine the Great, to Constantinople, whence they were removed to Milan, and ultimately by Renatus, or Reinold, Archbishop of Cologne, to the latter city, where they remain, and whence they have acquired the title of the Three Kings of Cologne.

OW is Christmas i-come,
  Father and Son together in One,
  Holy Ghost as ye be One,
    In fere-a
  God send us a good new year-a.

RELIGIOUS CAROLS.

I would now sing, for and I might,
Of a Child is fair to sight;
His mother Him bare this enders[1] night,
    So still-a;
And as it was His will-a.

There came three kings from Galilee,
To Bethlehem, that fair citie,
To see Him that should ever be
    By right-a;
Lord, and king, and knight-a.

As they came forth with their offering,
They met with Herod, that moody king,
He asked them of their coming
    This tide a;
And thus to them he said-a:—

"Of whence be ye, you kings three?"
"Of the East, as you may see,
To seek Him that should ever be
    By right-a;
Lord, and king, and knight-a."

"When you to this Child have been,
Come you home this way again,
Tell me the sights that ye have seen,
    I pray-a;
Go not another way-a."

[1] last.

RELIGIOUS CAROLS.

They took their leave both old and young,
Of Herod, that moody king;
They went forth with their offering,
  By light-a
Of the star that shone so bright-a.

Till they came into the place
Where Jesus and his mother was,
There they offered with great solace
  In fere-a;
Gold, incense, and myrrh-a.

When they had their offering made,
As the Holy Ghost them bade,
Then were they both merry and glad
  And light-a;
It was a good fair sight-a.

Anon, as on their way they went,
The Father of heaven an Angel sent,
To those three kings that made present,
  That day-a,
Who thus to them did say-a:—

"My Lord hath warned you every one,
By Herod king ye go not home,
For an you do, he will you slone[1]
  And strye-a,[2]
And hurt you wonderly-a."

[1] slay.   [2] stay.

RELIGIOUS CAROLS.

So forth they went another way,
Through the might of God, His lay[1]
As the Angel to them did say,
    Full right-a,
It was a good fair sight-a.

When they were come to their countree,
Merry and glad they were all three,
Of the sight that they had see
    By night-a;
By the star's shining light-a.

Kneel we now all here adown
To that Lord of great renown,
And pray we in good devotion
    For grace-a,
In Heaven to have a place-a.

A CAROL FOR THE EPIPHANY.

This is a well-known, although it cannot be styled a popular, carol, since, although it is included in every collection of carols, it is not found in any broadside that has fallen under notice, nor is it contained in Hone's list of such productions. It probably first appeared in Davies Gilbert's collection of Carols sung in the West of England; and next in Mr. Sandys's collection, where it is also given as a West-country carol, "for Christmas day in the morning." Mr. Sandys observes, in reference to the number

---

[1] law.

RELIGIOUS CAROLS.

of the shepherds, that "according to some legends the number was four, —called Misael, Achael, Cyriacus, and Stephanus, and these, with the names of the three kings, were used as a charm to cure the biting of serpents and other venomous reptiles and beasts. In the seventh of the Chester Mysteries, the shepherds, who are there but three, have the more homely names of Harvey, Trowle, and Tudd, and are Cheshire or Lancashire boors by birth and habits." Mr. Sandys is not quite accurate in the latter part of this statement. The shepherds in the Chester play to which he refers—"The Play of the Shepherds"—are four in number, who are severally designated as Primus, Secundus, and Tercius Pastor; but whose names appear from the dialogue to be Hancken, Harvey, and Tudd; and Trowle, who is a distinct person, always mentioned by name.

HE first Noël the Angel did say,
Was to three poor Shepherds in fields as they lay;
In fields where they lay keeping their sheep
In a cold winter's night that was so deep.[1]
    Noël, Noël, Noël, Noël,
    Born is the King of Israel.

They looked up and saw a Star
Shining in the East beyond them far,
And to the earth it gave great light,
And so continued both day and night.
    Noël, &c.

And by the light of that same Star,
Three Wise Men came from countries far;
To seek for a king was their intent,
And to follow the Star wherever it went.
    Noël, &c.

[1] This is the reading of every known copy, but it should probably be— "In a cold winter's night when the snow was so deep."

RELIGIOUS CAROLS.

This Star drew nigh to the North West,
O'er Bethlehem it took it's rest,
And there it did both stop and stay
Right over the place where Jesus lay.
      Noël, &c.

Then did they know assuredly
Within that house the King did lie:
One entered in then for to see,
But found the Babe in poverty.
      Noël, &c.

Then enter'd all the Wise Men three
Most reverently upon their knee,
And offer'd there in His presence,
Both gold, and myrrh, and frankincense.
      Noël, &c.

Between an ox-stall and an ass,
This Child there truly born He was;
For want of clothing they did Him lay
All in the manger among the hay.
      Noël, &c.

Now let us all with one accord
Sing praises to our heavenly Lord,
That did make heaven and earth of nought,
But with His blood mankind hath bought.
      Noël, &c.

If we in our time shall do well,
We shall be free from death and hell;

RELIGIOUS CAROLS.

> God hath prepared for us all,
> A resting place in general.
>   Noël, Noël, Noël, Noël,
>   Born is the King of Israel.

THE HOLLY AND THE IVY.

THIS carol appears to have nearly escaped the notice of collectors, as it has been reprinted by one alone, who states his copy to have been taken from " an old broadside, printed a century and a half since," i. e. about 1710. It is still retained on the broadsheets printed at Birmingham. It is possible that it is an ancient carol. The praise of the holly and ivy was a favourite subject with the mediæval carolists. The epithet " merry" is applied to the organ by Chaucer, in his Canterbury Tales, where, in a description of the possessions of a poor widow, the Nun's Priest is made to say :—

> " She had a cock, hight Chaunticleer,
> In all the land of crowing was none his peer:
> His voice was merrier than the *merry organ*
> On mass days that in the church goon."

But later writers almost invariably speak of the instrument in very different terms :—we have the " pealing organ" of Milton ; the " sacred organ" of Dryden ; the " deep" organ's " majestic sound" of Congreve ; the " deep-mouth'd organ" of Hughes ; and " the deep, majestic, solemn, organs" of Pope.

HE holly and the ivy
   Now are both well grown,
Of all the trees that are in the wood
   The holly bears the crown.

RELIGIOUS CAROLS.

Chorus.
The rising of the sun,
    The running of the deer,
The playing of the merry organ,
    The singing in the choir.

The holly bears a blossom
    As white as any flower,
And Mary bore sweet Jesus Christ
    To be our sweet Saviour.

The holly bears a berry
    As red as any blood,
And Mary bore sweet Jesus Christ
    To do poor sinners good.

The holly bears a prickle
    As sharp as any thorn,
And Mary bore sweet Jesus Christ
    On Christmas day in the morn.

The holly bears a bark
    As bitter as any gall,
And Mary bore sweet Jesus Christ
    For to redeem us all.

The holly and the ivy
    Now are both well grown,
Of all the trees that are in the wood
    The holly bears the crown.

THE TWELVE GOOD JOYS OF MARY.

This is one of the most popular of carols. The earliest known version is in a manuscript of the fourteenth century, where it is entitled "Joyes Fyve." The version called "The Seven Joys" (the first seven verses of that here given) is, and has been for a very long time past, annually reprinted by the printers of carol-sheets throughout the entire length and breadth of the land. The unfortunate poet's difficulty of finding a rhyme for "one" in the first verse has led him to use a rather singular expression; but we may be certain nothing irreverent was intended, and the text as it stands, homely though it be, appeals to the human heart much more forcibly than some modern alterations of it, such as,

> "To see our blessed Saviour
> Sit upon the throne;"

which, apart from the impropriety of making the sight of her holy Son in His glory, the *first* of the blessed Virgin's joys, puts wholly aside the incident which, if not all *men*, certainly all *women*, must admit naturally caused the Holy Mother her greatest happiness. The extension of the Seven joys to Twelve is confined to the northern parts of the country, being only found on broadsides printed at Newcastle late in the last, or early in the present century. In the present version the first seven verses are given from the older and most generally followed copies, the Newcastle version, whence the last five verses are taken, having corrupted the former portion of the carol to a very great extent. In its extended form the carol has never yet been given in any collection.

RELIGIOUS CAROLS.

HE first good joy our Mary had,
It was the joy of one,
To see her own Son Jesus
To suck at her breast bone;
To suck at her breast bone,
Good man, and blessed may he be,
Both Father, Son, and Holy Ghost,
To all eternity.

The next good joy our Mary had,
It was the joy of two,
To see her own son Jesus
To make the lame to go;
To make the lame to go,
Good man, &c.

The next good joy our Mary had,
It was the joy of three;
To see her own Son Jesus
To make the blind to see;
To make the blind to see,
Good man, &c.

The next good joy our Mary had,
It was the joy of four,
To see her own Son Jesus
To read the Bible o'er;
To read the Bible o'er,
Good man, &c.

RELIGIOUS CAROLS.

The next good joy our Mary had,
    It was the joy of five,
To see her own son Jesus
    To raise the dead alive;
To raise the dead alive,
        Good man, &c.

The next good joy our Mary had,
    It was the joy of six,
To see her own Son Jesus
    To wear the crucifix;
To wear the crucifix,
        Good man, &c.

The next good joy our Mary had,
    It was the joy of seven,
To see her own Son Jesus
    To wear the crown of Heaven;
To wear the crown of Heaven,
        Good man, &c.

The next good joy our Mary had,
    It was the joy of eight,
To see our blessed Saviour
    Turn darkness into light;
Turn darkness into light,
        Good man, &c.

The next good joy our Mary had,
    It was the joy of nine,

RELIGIOUS CAROLS.

To see our blessed Saviour
 Turn water into wine;
Turn water into wine,
 Good man, &c.

The next good joy our Mary had,
 It was the joy of ten,
To see our blessed Saviour
 Write without a pen;
Write without a pen,
 Good man, &c.

The next good joy our Mary had,
 It was the joy of eleven,
To see our blessed Saviour
 Shew the gates of Heaven;
Shew the gates of Heaven,
 Good man, &c.

The next good joy our Mary had,
 It was the joy of twelve,
To see our blessed Saviour
 Shut close the gates of hell;
Shut close the gates of hell,
  Good man, and blessed may he be,
  Both Father, Son, and Holy Ghost,
   To all eternity.

THE HOLY WELL.

THE broadside printers almost invariably describe this as "A Very Ancient Carol," and in so doing they are, unquestionably, not far wrong. The legend dates back, no doubt, to Pre-Reformation times, when such tales were invented by the priests to satisfy the cravings of the common people for more detailed particulars of the life of our Blessed Lord than the Holy Scriptures afforded; but the composition of the carol may be ascribed, with reasonable probability, to the latter half of the sixteenth century, to the ballads of which period it bears a strong resemblance in point of style. The carol is now printed from a sheet copy published during the last century, on which it is described as "A Carol on Christ's Humility to Sinners." There are some touches in this carol which point out with remarkable clearness the class of persons to whom it was addressed; such, for instance, as the coupling with the permission to the Child to go to play the injunction to "behave" Himself; the pride of the "lords' and ladies' sons," and the wounded feelings of the Boy at their haughty rejection of His offer. The carol has a widely spread popularity. On a broadside copy printed at Gravesend there is placed immediately under the title a woodcut purporting to be a representation of "The Site of the Holy Well, Palestine;" but the admiration excited thereby for the excellent good taste of the printer is too soon, alas! dispelled, for between the second and third stanzas we see another woodcut representing a feather clad and crowned negro seated on a barrel smoking;—a veritable ornament of a tobacconist's paper. One almost wonders at the omission of the usual accompanying conundrum.

S it fell out one May morning,
  And upon a bright holiday,
 Sweet Jesus asked of His dear Mother,
  If He might go to play.

RELIGIOUS CAROLS.

"To play, to play, sweet Jesus shall go,
And to play now get you gone,
And let me hear of no complaint,
At night when you come home."

Sweet Jesus went down to yonder town,
As far as the Holy Well,
And there did see as fine children
As any tongue can tell.

And he said, "God bless you every one,
And your bodies Christ save and see;
Little children, shall I play with you?
And you shall play with Me."

But they made answer to Him, "No,"
They were lords' and ladies' sons;
And He was but a maiden's child,
Born in an ox's stall.

Sweet Jesus turned him round about,
And He neither laugh'd nor smil'd,
But the tears came trickling from His eyes
Like water from the skies.

Sweet Jesus turned Him round about,
To His Mother dear home went He,
And said, "I have been in yonder town,
As after you may see.

RELIGIOUS CAROLS.

"I have been down in yonder town,
As far as the Holy Well;
And there did I meet with as fine children
As any tongue can tell.

"And I bid God bless them every one,
And their bodies Christ save and see;
Little children, shall I play with you?
And you shall play with Me.

"But then they answered Me, 'No,'
They were lords' and ladies' sons;
And I was but a maiden's child,
Born in an ox's stall."

"Though You are but a maiden's child,
Born in an ox's stall,
Thou art the Christ, the King of Heaven,
And the Saviour of them all.

"Sweet Jesus, go down into yonder town,
And as far as the Holy Well,
And take away those sinful souls,
And dip them deep in hell."

"Nay, nay," sweet Jesus mildly said,
"Nay, nay, that may not be,
For there are too many sinful souls
Crying out for the help of Me."

RELIGIOUS CAROLS.

O then spoke the Angel Gabriel,
Upon one sure set steven,[1]
"Although you are but a maiden's child,
You are the King of Heaven."

DIVES AND LAZARUS.

THIS carol is included in Hone's list of carols in his possession which were in use at the period he wrote—1822; but it was never printed in any collection until 1860. Hone speaks of the ludicrous effect produced by the thirteenth verse, "when the metre of the last line is solemnly drawn out to its utmost length by a Warwickshire chanter, and as solemnly listened to by the well-disposed crowd, who seem, without difficulty, to believe that Dives sits on a serpent's *knee*." "The idea of sitting on the knee," he adds, "was perhaps conveyed to the *poet's* mind by old woodcut representations of Lazarus seated in Abraham's lap. More anciently, Abraham was frequently drawn holding him up by the sides, to be seen by Dives in hell. In an old book [Postilla Guillermi, 4to. Basil, 1491] they are so represented, with the addition of a devil blowing the fire under Dives with a pair of bellows." The idea may have been conveyed to the writer's mind as Hone suggests, or it may be that the *serpent's* knee was only thought of as antithetical to the *Angel's* knee on which Lazarus was to rest. The carol is now given from a sheet copy printed at Worcester in the last century. The composition is much in the style of a sixteenth century ballad, but the last verse conveys an idea of greater antiquity, as it seems to give expression to the opinion that the devotion of worldly goods to pious or charitable uses sufficed to avert future punishment. There can be little, if any, doubt of this being the piece referred to in Fletcher's comedy of "Monsieur Thomas," where a fiddler is introduced, enumerating the songs he can sing, amongst which is "the merry ballad of Dives and Lazarus."

---

[1] appointed time.

RELIGIOUS CAROLS.

S it fell out upon a day,
　　Rich Dives made a feast,
And he invited all his guests,
　　And gentry of the best.

Then Lazarus laid him down, and down,
　　And down at Dives's door,
"Some meat, some drink, brother Dives,
　　Bestow upon the poor."

"Thou art none of my brother, Lazarus,
　　That lies begging at my door,
No meat nor drink will I give thee,
　　Nor bestow upon the poor."

Then Lazarus laid him down, and down,
　　And down at Dives's wall,
"Some meat, some drink, brother Dives,
　　Or with hunger starve I shall."

"Thou art none of my brother, Lazarus,
　　That lies begging at my wall,
No meat nor drink will I give thee,
　　But with hunger starve you shall."

Then Lazarus laid him down, and down,
　　And down at Dives's gate,
"Some meat, some drink, brother Dives,
　　For Jesus Christ His sake."

RELIGIOUS CAROLS.

"Thou art none of my brother, Lazarus,
   That lies begging at my gate,
No meat nor drink I'll give to thee,
   For Jesus Christ His sake."

Then Dives sent out his merry men
   To whip poor Lazarus away,
But they had no power to strike a stroke,
   And flung their whips away.

Then Dives sent out his hungry dogs
   To bite him as he lay,
But they had no power to bite at all,
   So licked his sores away.

As it fell out upon a day,
   Poor Lazarus sickened and died,
There came an Angel out of heaven,
   His soul there for to guide.

"Rise up, rise up, brother Lazarus,
   And come along with me,
For there's a place in heaven provided
   To sit on an Angel's knee."

As it fell out upon a day,
   Rich Dives sickened and died,
There came a serpent out of hell,
   His soul there for to guide.

RELIGIOUS CAROLS.

"Rise up, rise up, brother Dives,
    And come along with me,
For there's a place in hell provided
    To sit on a serpent's knee."

Then Dives, lifting his eyes to heaven,
    And seeing poor Lazarus blest,
"Give me a drop of water, brother Lazarus,
    To quench my flaming thirst.

"Oh! had I as many years to abide,
    As there are blades of grass,
Then there would be an ending day;
    But in hell I must ever last.

"Oh! was I now but alive again,
    For the space of one half hour,
I would make my will and then secure
    That the devil should have no power."

THE CARNAL AND THE CRANE.

ALTHOUGH no copies of this carol of an earlier date than the middle of the last century have been met with, there is sufficient internal evidence to prove that it is of considerable age. The Crane has long ceased to be a visitant to this country, although formerly it abounded here, and was highly prized as a table dainty on account of the savour and delicacy of its flesh. At the inthronization of George Nevell, Archbishop of York, in the reign of Edward IV, no fewer than 204 cranes were brought to table. In the "Northumberland Household Book," 1512, one of the regulations concerning the purveyance of provisions runs thus:—"It is

RELIGIOUS CAROLS.

thought that Cranys muste be hadde at Crystynmas and other principal Feestes for my Lordes own Mees so they be bought at xvjd a pece." Legislative attempts were made in the reigns of Henry VIII and Edward VI to preserve these birds by the imposition of a penalty of 20d. for every crane's egg taken and destroyed. The crane chiefly frequented the fenlands of Lincolnshire and Cambridgeshire, and it is probably to the drainage and inclosure of those lands that the present absence of the bird from England is to be attributed. Thus much for the Crane ;—but what was the Carnal? The word is not to be found in any dictionary of old and obsolete words which has been consulted; neither does it occur in any other composition than this carol. Hone, in noticing this carol, says merely, "The Carnal is a bird." It may possibly, having regard to the place and company in which it is found, be considered as a not too far-fetched conjecture, to suppose it to have been one of those river-birds, such as the heron or stork, which feed on flesh as well as fish, and which, from such flesh-eating habits, acquired its peculiar name. The introduction of the legend of the cock, which also occurs in the earlier carol on St. Stephen's day, is strong confirmation of the opinion as to the antiquity of this carol. Hone calls it a Warwickshire carol, but it seems more probable that it had its origin in a more eastern part of the country. The oldest broadsides known were printed at Worcester. The obsolete word "renne," or "rein," i. e. " to run," used in the second line, is corrupted by the broadside printers into "reign" and "range."

S I passed by a river side,
  And there as I did rein,
  In argument I chanced to hear
   A Carnal and a Crane.

  The Carnal said unto the Crane,
   "Sure all the world will turn,
  Before we had the Father,
   But now we have the Son!

RELIGIOUS CAROLS.

"Whence does the Son come from?
 From where and from what place?"
"Out of the land of Egypt,
 Between an ox and an ass!"

"I pray thee," said the Carnal,
 "Tell me before thou goest;
Was not the Mother of Jesus
 Conceived by the Holy Ghost?"

"She was the purest Virgin,
 And the cleanest from all sin;
She was the handmaid of the Lord,
 And the Mother of our King."

"Where is the golden cradle
 That Christ was rocked in?
Where are the silken sheets
 That Jesus was wrapt in?"

"A Manger was the cradle
 That Christ was rocked in;
The provender the asses left,
 So sweetly he slept in.

There was a Star in the East land,
 So bright it did appear
Into King Herod's chamber,
 And where King Herod were.

RELIGIOUS CAROLS.

"The Wise Men soon espied it,
    And told the King on high,
A princely babe was born that night
    No prince should e'er destroy.

"'If this be true,' King Herod said,
    'As thou tellest me,
This roasted cock that lies in the dish
    Shall crow full fences[1] three.'

"The cock soon freshly feathered was,
    By the work of God's own hand,
And then three fences crowed he,
    In the dish where he did stand.

"'Rise up, rise up, you merry men all,
    See that you ready be,
All children under two years old
    Now slaughtered shall be.'

"Then Jesus, aye and Joseph,
    And Mary that was so pure,
They travelled into Egypt land,
    As you shall find most sure.

"And when they came to Egypt land,
    Among some fierce wild beasts,
Mary, grown quite weary,
    Must needs sit down to rest.

        [1] shouts (?).

RELIGIOUS CAROLS.

"'Come sit thee down,' says Jesus,
    'Come sit thee down by Me,
And thou shalt see that these wild beasts
    Will come and worship Me.'

"First came the lovely lion,
    Which Jesus's grace did bring,
And of the wild beasts in the field,
    The lion shall be king.

"We'll choose our virtuous princes,
    Of birth and high degree,
In every nation of the world,
    Where'er we come and see.

"Then Jesus, aye and Joseph,
    And Mary that was unknown,
They passed by a husbandman,
    As he his seed had sown.

"'God speed thee, man!' said Jesus,
    'Go fetch thy ox and wain,
And carry home thy corn again,
    Which thou this day hath sown.'

"The husbandman fell on his knees,
    Even before His face;
And made a lowly reverence
    To Jesus Christ His grace.

RELIGIOUS CAROLS.

"' Long time hast Thou been looked for,
  But now Thou art come at last;
And I myself do now believe,
  Thy name is Jesus called.'

"' The truth, man, thou hast spoken,
  Of it thou may'st be sure,
For I must shed My precious blood
  For thee and thousands more.

"' If any one should come this way,
  And inquire for Me alone,
Tell them that Jesus passed by,
  As thou thy seed had sown.'

" After that there came King Herod,
  With his train most furiously,
Inquiring of the husbandman,
  Whether Jesus passed by.

"' Why the truth it must be spoken,
  And the truth it must be known,
For Jesus passed by this way,
  As I my seed had sown.

"' And now I have it reapen,
  And some laid on my wain,
The other you see is fit to carry
  Into my barns again.

RELIGIOUS CAROLS.

"' Turn back,' said the Captain of the guard,
   ' Your labour and mine's in vain,
It's full three quarters of a year
   Since he his seed has sown.'

" So Herod was deceived
   By the work of God's own hand,
And further he proceeded
   Into the Holy Land.

" There were thousands of children young,
   Who for His sake did die;
Do not forbid these little ones,
   And do not them deny.

" The truth now I have spoken,
   And the truth now I have shown;
Thus the blessed Virgin
   Brought forth our Lord the Son."

THE MIRACLES OF CHRIST.

The following simple, but characteristic, production is found only on broadsides printed at Devonport for circulation in Devonshire, Cornwall, and Monmouthshire. It seems not unworthy of preservation as a specimen of the style of composition which arrests the attention and excites the sympathy of the peasants and miners of those counties at the present time. It is now printed for the first time in a collection.

HEN Jesus the Lord
    Came down to our earth,
He meanly was clad,
    And low was His birth:
Though Lord of creation,
    And Ruler above,
He chose in a station
    Most humble to move.

His life was all toil
    When with us below,
Diseases He cured,
    And softened our woe:
A friend to the friendless
    He ever was found;
His blessings were endless
    To sinners around.

RELIGIOUS CAROLS.

The lepers He cleansed,
   The deaf heard His voice,
The dumb spoke His praise,
   And were made to rejoice:
The dead Jesus raised
   To life from the grave;
His name then be praised,
   Whose end was to save.

THE SEVEN VIRGINS.

THIS carol appeared for the first time in a collection in "A Garland of Christmas Carols, Ancient and Modern," published in 1860, the editor of which says, "This is another Carol which has hitherto eluded the search of all collectors of such religious antiquities. The legend is extremely ancient. The line towards the end which alludes to 'our king and queen' is evidently a modern interpolation. The metre, occasionally faulty, is here given just as it occurs on the original old Birmingham broadside."

LL under the leaves, and the leaves of life,
   I met with virgins seven,
And one of them was Mary mild,
   Our Lord's mother of heaven.

" O what are you seeking, you seven fair maids,
   All under the leaves of life,
Come tell, come tell, what seek you,
   All under the leaves of life?"

RELIGIOUS CAROLS.

"We're seeking for no leaves, Thomas,
    But for a friend of thine,
We're seeking for sweet Jesus Christ,
    To be our guide and thine."

"Go down, go down to yonder town,
    And sit in the gallery,
And there you'll see sweet Jesus Christ,
    Nailed to a big yew tree."

So down they went to yonder town,
    As fast as foot could fall,
And many a grievous bitter tear
    From the virgins' eyes did fall.

"O peace, mother, O peace, mother,
    Your weeping doth me grieve,
I must suffer this," he said,
    "For Adam and for Eve.

"O mother, take you John Evangelist,
    All for to be your son,
And he will comfort you sometimes,
    Mother, as I have done."

"O come, thou John Evangelist,
    Thou'rt welcome unto me,
But more welcome my own dear Son,
    Whom I nursed on my knee."

RELIGIOUS CAROLS.

Then He laid His head on His right shoulder,
    Seeing death it struck Him nigh,—
"The Holy Ghost be with your soul,
    I die, mother dear, I die."

O the rose, the gentle rose,
    And the fennel that grows so green,
God give us grace, in every place,
    To pray for our king and queen.

Furthermore for our enemies all
    Our prayers they should be strong,
Amen, good Lord; your Charity
    Is the ending of my song.

A NEW DIAL.

This is found on the leaf of an old almanack, published about 1625, and preserved in the British Museum. The number, Twelve, that of the Apostles, was very suggestive to the old carolists.

1 ONE God, one Baptism, and one Faith,
    One Truth there is, the Scripture saith.

2 Two Testaments (the Old and New)
    We do acknowledge to be true.

RELIGIOUS CAROLS.

3 Three persons are in Trinity,
   Which make One God in Unity.

4 Four sweet Evangelists there are,
   Christ's birth, life, death, which do declare.

5 Five senses (like five kings) maintain
   In every man a several reign.

6 Six days to labour, is not wrong,
   For God Himself did work so long.

7 Seven Liberal Arts hath God sent down,
   With Divine skill man's soul to crown.

8 Eight in Noah's Ark alive were found,
   When (in a word) the world lay drowned.

9 Nine Muses (like the heaven's nine spheres)
   With sacred tunes entice our ears.

10 Ten Statutes God to Moses gave,
    Which kept or broke, do spill or save.

11 Eleven with Christ in Heaven do dwell,
    The Twelfth for ever burns in Hell.

12 Twelve are attending on God's Son,
    Twelve make our Creed. The Dial's done.

    Count One the first hour of thy Birth,
    The hours that follow lead to Earth;
    Count Twelve thy doleful striking knell,
    And then thy Dial shall go well.

MAN'S DUTY;

OR, MEDITATION FOR THE TWELVE HOURS OF THE DAY.

This is a more modern version of the preceding carol.

NE God there is of wisdom, glory, might;
One Faith there is to guide our souls aright;
One Truth there is for man to practise in;
One Baptism to cleanse our souls from sin.

Two Testaments there are, the Old and New,
In which the Law and Gospel thou may'st view;
The one for works and deeds doth precepts give,
The other saith the just by faith shall live.

Three Persons in the glorious Trinity
Make one true God in perfect unity,
The Father, Son, and Holy Ghost, those three
For ever equal and eternal be.

Four most divine and righteous holy men
They did the life of our Redeemer pen,
They were Matthew, Mark, and Luke, and John likewise,
Whose righteous truth let every Christian prize.

RELIGIOUS CAROLS.

Five scuses do in every man maintain
A governing power, rule and reign ;
The hearing, seeing, tasting, feeling, smelling,
Which at thy death will leave thee and thy dwelling.

Six days, O man, thou hast to labour in,
So merciful and good thy God hath been,
Of seven unto Himself He took but one,
O rob Him not of that to leave Him none.

Seven Liberal Arts, by a divine decree,
Unto man's knowing soul united be,
Rhetoric, grammar, music and geometry,
Arithmetic, logic, and astronomy.

Eight persons in the ark of Noah were
When God He would the world no longer spare ;
Sin did abound, therefore all flesh He drown'd
Which in that ship of safety were not bound.

Nine Muses their harmonious voices raise
To sing our blessed dear Redeemer's praise,
Who is the spring from whence all blessings flow
To us poor living mortals here below.

There are Commandments Ten we should obey,
And yet how apt we are to go astray,
Leaving them all our folly to pursue,
As if we did not care what God could do.

RELIGIOUS CAROLS.

Eleven disciples did with Jesus pray
When Judas did our Saviour Christ betray,
Though, covetous for greedy gain, he fell
To be perdition's child condemned to hell.

Twelve Tribes there were amongst our fathers old,
Twelve Articles our Christian faith does hold,
Twelve Gates in New Jerusalem there be,
Unto which city Christ bring you and me.

CHRISTMAS CAROLS.

PART II.

FESTIVE CAROLS AND SONGS.

"Tis merry in Hall
When beards wagge all."
Old Song, quoted by SHAKSPERE.

CAROLS ON BRINGING IN THE BOAR'S HEAD.

THE head of a wild boar formed, at a very early period of our history, the principal and choicest dish at all great feasts, and especially at Christmas. Why it should have been so highly esteemed we cannot now tell; but possibly the danger encountered in attacking so ferocious an animal as the wild boar, and the consequent importance attaching to it when slain, as a trophy of victory, may have had an influence in raising it to the position it enjoyed. The boar's head was brought to table with great ceremony; trumpeters preceded the bearer, sounding, and various other persons attended and formed a procession. Holinshed, in his Chronicle, acquaints us how King Henry II. on the occasion of the coronation of his son Henry, as heir apparent, on the 15th June, 1170, himself brought up the boar's head, with trumpets before it. At Queen's College, Oxford, founded in 1340, the custom of bringing in a boar's head, on Christmas Day, with music and a carol (given hereinafter), has been preserved to our own times. At Henry VI.'s coronation boars' heads were placed on the table in "castellys of golde and enamell." Margaret, daughter of Henry VII, and wife to James IV. of Scotland, "at the furst course" of her wedding dinner, "was served of a wyld borres hed gylt, within a fayr platter." In the household accounts of King Henry VIII. we find an entry on 24th November, 1529, of a payment to a servant of the Lord Chamberlain of 40s. " in rewarde for bringing a wylde bore unto the king," and on the last day of December in the same year, a like sum of 40s. was paid to one of the Lord Chamberlain's servants for a similar service. A servant of "Maister Tresorer" received 4s. 8d. on 18th December, 1531, "for bringing a wylde bore's head to the king." The custom continued through-

FESTIVE CAROLS

out the reign of Elizabeth,—during which, on Christmas Day, in the Inner Temple, "a fair and large boar's head" was served "upon a silver platter with minstrelsy;"—and into the reigns of her immediate successors, for Aubrey, in a manuscript, dated 1678, says: "Before the last civil wars, in gentlemen's houses at Christmass, the first diet that was brought to table was a boar's head with a lemon in his mouth."

The following is a collection of the principal, if not the only, Boar's head carols now extant:—

I.

THIS is the earliest known carol of the kind. It is contained in a manuscript of the fifteenth century.

<blockquote>
Hey! Hey! Hey! Hey!
The Boar his head is armèd gay.
</blockquote>

HE boar his head in hand I bring
With garland gay in porttoring,[1]
I pray you all with me to sing,
    With Hey!

Lords, knights, and squires,
Parsons, priests, and vicars,
The boar his head is the first mess,[2]
    With Hey!

The boar his head, as I you say,
He takes his leave and goeth his way,
Gone after the Twelfth day,
    With Hey!

[1] This word is not in any Glossary.   [2] dish.

AND SONGS.

Then comes in the second course with mickle¹ pride,
The cranes, the herons, the bitterns, by their side
The partridges and the plovers, the woodcocks, and the snipe,
   With Hey!

Larks in hot show ladies for to pick,
Good drink thereto, luscious and fine,
Blwet of Allemaine,² Romnay,³ and wine,
   With Hey!

Good brewed ale and wine, dare I well say,
The boar his head with mustard armèd so gay,
Furmity for pottage, with venison fine,
And the umbles of the doe and all that ever comes in,
Capons well baked, with the pieces of the roe,
Raisins of currants, with other spices mo.⁴
   With Hey!

II.

This is from the manuscript of the fifteenth century which was edited, as before mentioned, in 1847, for the Percy Society by Mr. Thomas Wright.

IDINGS I bring you for to tell,
What me in wild forest befel,
When me must with a wild beast mell⁵
With a boar so bryme.⁶

¹ much.   ² German wines.   ³ a Spanish wine.   ⁴ more.
   ⁵ meddle.   ⁶ fierce.

FESTIVE CAROLS

A boar so bryme that me pursued,
Me for to kill so sharply moved,
That brymly beast so cruel and unrude, [1]
    There tamed I him,
And reft from him both life and limb.

Truly, to show you that this is true,
His head with my sword I hew,
To make this day to you mirth new,
    Now eat thereof anon.

Eat, and much good do it you;
Take your bread and mustard thereto.
Joy with me that I have thus done,
I pray you be glad every one,
    And joy all in one.

III.

This is from the same manuscript as the preceding.

    Po, po, po, po,
    [I] love brawn and so do mo.

T the beginning of the meat
Of a boar's head ye shall eat,
And in the mustard ye shall wet
    And ye shall singen[2] ere ye go.

[1] savage.   [2] the old form of the plural.

AND SONGS.

Welcome be ye that be here,
And ye shall have right good cheer,
And also a right good fare,
    And ye shall singen ere ye go.

Welcome be ye every one,
For ye shall sing right anon;
Hie ye fast that ye had done,
    And ye shall singen ere ye go.

IV.

THIS carol is contained on a single leaf, all that is known of the collection of which it formed part, which formerly belonged to Thomas Hearne, the antiquary, and is now preserved in the Bodleian Library at Oxford. Fortunately this leaf contains the colophon, which runs thus:—" Thus endeth the Christmasse carolles, newely inprinted at Londō, in the fletestrete, at the sygne of the sonne, by Wynkyn de Worde. The yere of our lorde M.D.xxi." The carol is entitled, "A caroll bringyng in the bores heed."

    Caput Apri defero
    Reddens laudes Domino.

HE boar's head in hand bring I,
    With garlands gay and rosemary;
    I pray you all sing merrily,
        Qui estis in convivio.

FESTIVE CAROLS

The boar's head, I understand,
Is the chief service in this land;
Look wherever it be found,
  Servite cum cantico.

Be glad, lords, both more or less,
 For this hath ordained our steward
To cheer you all this Christmas,
 The boar's head with mustard.

V.

This is a modernized version of the preceding carol, and owes its chief interest to the circumstance of its being still annually sung on Christmas Day at Queen's College, Oxford, where the custom of bringing the boar's head to table on that day has been uninterruptedly maintained. The new version was in all probability made and introduced into use about the commencement of the last century, as it is palpably referred to by Hearne in a note on the older carol, which he printed amongst the "Notæ et Spicilegium," appended to his edition of William of Newbury's Chronicle in 1719, stating that "it will be perceived how much the same carol is altered as it is sung in some places even now from what it was at first." The ceremony now attending the bringing in the boar's head at Queen's College is as follows:—The head (the finest and largest that can be procured) is decorated with garlands, bays, and rosemary, and is borne into the Hall on the shoulders of two of the chief servants of the college, and followed by members of the college, and by the college choir. The carol is sung by a member (usually a fellow) of the college, and the chorus by the choir as the procession advances to the high table, on reaching which, the boar's head is placed before the Provost, who sends slices of it to those who are with him at the high table; and the head is then sent round to the other tables in the hall and partaken of by the

AND SONGS.

occupants.[1] The music to which the carol is sung (a kind of chant) may be seen in the appendix to this collection of carols. Some years since it was more than once stated in print that the boar's head had given way to a carved wooden substitute, but there is no reason whatever for believing that such an absurdity was ever permitted. There was an amusing tradition formerly current in Oxford concerning the boar's head custom, which represented that usage as a commemoration of an act of valour performed by a student of the college, who, while walking in the neighbouring forest of Shotover and reading Aristotle, was suddenly attacked by a wild boar. The furious beast came open-mouthed upon the youth, who, however, very courageously, and with a happy presence of mind, thrust the volume he was reading down the boar's throat, crying, "Græcum est," and fairly choked the savage with the sage. This tradition, together with the customary celebration, occasioned the production of the following song, which appeared in "The Oxford Sausage," a miscellany of humorous poetry relating to Oxford, published nearly a century ago, under the care of the Rev. Thomas Warton, who himself largely contributed to it.

"SONG

IN HONOUR OF THE CELEBRATION OF THE BOAR'S HEAD, AT QUEEN'S COLLEGE, OXFORD.

' *Tam Marti quam Mercurio.*'

"I sing not of Roman or Grecian mad games,
The Pythian, Olympic, and such like hard names;
Your patience awhile with submission I beg;
I strive but to honour the feast of *Coll. Reg.*
      Derry down, down, down, derry down.

---

[1] For the communication of these particulars the editor is indebted to the courtesy of the Rev. Dr. Jackson, Provost of Queen's College.

"No Thracian brawls at our rites eer prevail,
We temper our mirth with plain sober mild ale;
The tricks of old Circe deter us from wine;
Though we honour a *boar*, we won't make ourselves *swine*.
      Derry down, &c.

"Great Milo was famous for slaying his ox,
Yet he prov'd but an ass in cleaving of blocks;
But we had a hero for all things was fit,
Our motto displays both his valour and wit.
      Derry down, &c.

"Stout Hercules labour'd and look'd mighty big,
When he slew the half-starv'd Erymanthian pig;
But we can relate such a stratagem taken,
That the stoutest of *boars* could not *save his own bacon*.
      Derry down, &c.

"So dreadful this bristle-back'd foe did appear,
You'd have sworn he had got the wrong *pig by the ear*;
But instead of avoiding the mouth of the beast,
He ramm'd in a volume, and cried— *Græcum est.*
      Derry down, &c.

"In this gallant action such fortitude shewn is,
As proves him no coward, nor tender Adonis;
No armour but logic, by which we may find
That logic's the bulwark of body and mind.
      Derry down, &c.

"Ye, squires, that fear neither hills nor rough rocks,
And think you're full wise when you outwit a fox;
Enrich your poor brains, and expose them no more,
Learn Greek, and seek glory from hunting the *boar*.
      Derry down, &c."

AND SONGS.

The present copy of the carol is given from Dibdin's edition of "Ames's Typographical Antiquities," ii. 252.

HE boar's head in hand bear I,
Bedeck'd with bays and rosemary;
And I pray you, my masters, be merry,
  Quot estis in convivio.
   Caput Apri defero,
   Reddens laudes Domino.

The boar's head, as I understand,
Is the rarest dish in all this land,
Which thus bedeck'd with a gay garland,
  Let us *servire cantico.*
   Caput Apri defero,
   Reddens laudes Domino.

Our steward hath provided this
In honour of the King of bliss;
Which on this day to be served is
  In Reginensi Atrio.
   Caput Apri defero,
   Reddens laudes Domino.

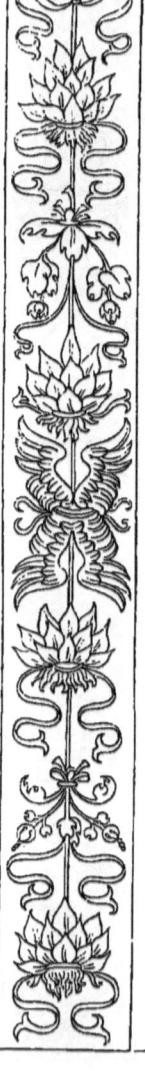

VI.

This carol is contained in a manuscript, formerly in the possession of Ritson, the antiquary, but now preserved amongst the additional manuscripts in the British Museum, which was written in the reign of Henry VIII. In addition to the words, the manuscript gives the music written for the carol, by a composer named Richard Smert, called elsewhere in the same manuscript, "Ricard Smert de Plymptre." This is in two parts (soprano and alto), with a chorus in three parts (soprano and two altos), and has been printed in John Stafford Smith's "Musica Antiqua," i. 22. The name of the author of the words is not recorded. Ritson, who printed the carol in his "Ancient Songs and Ballads," says, "*Nowel, Nowel* (the old French name for Christmas), and a great cry at that period, was the usual burden to this sort of things. It was likewise the name of this sort of composition, which is equally ancient and popular. Books of carols were cried about the streets of Paris in the thirteenth century. 'Noel, Noel, *à moult grant cris.*'"

Noel, Noel, Noel, Noel,
Tidings good I think to tell.

HE boar's head, that we bring here,
Betokeneth a prince without peer
Is born this day to buy us dear,
    Noel.

A boar is a sovereign beast,
And acceptable in every feast;
So might this Lord be to most[1] and least,
    Noel.

[1] greatest.

AND SONGS.

The boar's head we bring with song,
In worship of Him that thus sprung
Of a Virgin to redress all wrong;
        Noel.

VII.

THIS carol was sung, in 1607, at the ceremony of bringing in the Boar's Head before the Christmas Prince, a kind of Lord of Misrule, or Master of Revels, formerly annually elected from amongst the juniors of St. John the Baptist's College, Oxford, to preside during the Christmas holidays. This custom had prevailed in other Oxford colleges, particularly in Merton College, before the Reformation, when it was abolished. In the Societies of the Law, particularly Gray's Inn and the Temple, it continued long afterwards. "At a Christmas celebrated in the Hall of the Middle Temple, in the year 1635, the jurisdiction, privileges, and parade of this mock monarch are thus circumstantially described. He was attended by his Lord Keeper, Lord Treasurer, with eight white slaves, a captain of his Band of Pensioners, and of his Guard; and with two chaplains, who were so seriously impressed with an idea of his regal dignity, that when they preached before him on the preceding Sunday in the Temple Church, on ascending the pulpit they saluted him with three low bows. He dined, both in the Hall and in his privy chamber, under a cloth of estate. The pole-axes for his Gentlemen Pensioners were borrowed of Lord Salisbury. Lord Holland, his temporary Justice in Eyre, supplies him with venison on demand; and the Lord Mayor and Sheriffs of London with wine. On Twelfth Day, at going to church, he received many petitions, which he gave to his Master of Requests: and, like other kings, he had a favourite, whom, with others, gentlemen of high quality, he knighted at returning from church. [The satire conveyed in this last action, was, doubtless, keenly relished at the time.] His expenses, all from his own purse, amounted to two thousand pounds."

The change from the manners and tastes of the times when the former carols were written appears strikingly in the present production. Instead

FESTIVE CAROLS

of references to the Blessed Virgin and the King of bliss, we have the quasi-classic allusions to Meleager (the destroyer of the famed boar of Calydon), Ceres and Bacchus, so strongly characteristic of the age. It may be remarked that in all these carols, save one or two, mustard is mentioned as an accompaniment to the boar's head, in a manner that exalts it to an almost equal consequence with the head itself. It is alluded to as an essential article even so late as the eighteenth century, in the following passage from Dr. William King's poem, "The Art of Cookery:"—

> "At Christmas time.———
> Then if you would send up the Brawner's head,
> Sweet rosemary and bays around it spread;
> His foaming tusks let some large pippin grace,
> Or, midst these thundering spears an orange place;
> Sauce, like himself, offensive to its foes,
> The roguish mustard, dangerous to the nose.
> Sack and the well-spic'd Hippocras the wine,
> Wassail the bowl with ancient ribbons fine,
> Porridge with plums, and turkies with the chine."

HE Boar is dead,
  Lo, here is his head:
    What man could have done more
    Than his head off to strike,
  Meleager like,
    And bring it as I do before?

He living spoiled
Where good men toiled,
  Which made kind Ceres sorry;
But now, dead and drawn,
Is very good brawn,
  And we have brought it for ye.

AND SONGS.

Then set down the swineyard,
The foe to the vineyard,
　Let Bacchus crown his fall;
Let this boar's head and mustard
Stand for pig, goose, and custard,
　And so you are welcome all.

CAROL FOR CHRISTMAS DAY.

THIS carol is from the before-mentioned manuscript, formerly Ritson's, and now in the British Museum, of the early part of Henry VIII.'s reign. It has the peculiarity of having scraps of French incorporated into it, and this may perhaps point to the period at which Henry met Francis I. on the celebrated "Field of the Cloth of Gold," as that of its production. The music, in three parts (soprano, alto, and tenor), which accompanies the carol in the manuscript, will be found in John Stafford Smith's "Musica Antiqua," i. 26.

OEL, Noel, Noel, Noel,
　　Who is there, that singeth so, Noel,
　　　　　　Noel, Noel?

I am here, Sir Christhismas,
Welcome, my lord Sir Christhismas,
Welcome to all both more and less;¹
　　　　　Come near, Noel.

Dieu vous garde, beau Sire, tidings I you bring,
A maid hath born a Child full young,
The which causeth for to sing,
　　　　　Noel.

¹ great and small.

FESTIVE CAROLS

Christ is now born of a pure maid,
In an ox stall He is laid,
Wherefore sing we all at a braid,[1]
     Noel.

Buvez bien par toute la compagnie,
Make good cheer and be right merry,
And sing with us now joyfully,
     Noel.

HOLLY AND IVY.

THE custom of decking houses with evergreens about the close of the year is of Pagan origin, and was adopted by the Christians. It long since obtained a firm hold in England. In many of the Churchwarden's accounts in London parishes we meet with charges like the following :—

"Holme and Ivy at Christmas Eve, iiij *d.*"   *St. Mary at Hill.*
"It'm for Holly and Ivy at Christmas, ij *d. ob.*"   *St. Martin Outwich,*
 A. D. 1524.
"Paid for Holly and Ivye at Christmas, ij *d.*"   *Ibid.*, A. D. 1525.

The following carol is from a manuscript of the fifteenth century :—

OLLY and Ivy made a great party,
 Who should have the mastery
   In lands where they go.

   [1] suddenly.

AND SONGS.

Then spake Holly, "I am fierce and jolly,
I will have the mastery
>> In lands where we go."

Then spake Ivy, "I am loud and proud,
And I will have the mastery
>> In lands where we go."

Then spake Holly, and set him down on his knee,
"I pray thee, gentle Ivy,
Say[1] me no villany
>> In lands where we go."

HERE COMES HOLLY.

THIS is from the same manuscript as the preceding.

>> Alleluia, Alleluia,
>> Alleluia, now sing we.

ERE comes Holly that is so gent,[2]
To please all men is his intent.
>> Alleluia.

But Lord and Lady of this hall,
Whosoever against Holly call.
>> Alleluia.

[1] essay, do.   [2] gallant, pretty.

FESTIVE CAROLS

Whosoever against Holly do cry,
In a lepe[1] he shall hang full high.
     Alleluia.

Whosoever against Holly do sing,
He may weep and hands wring.
     Alleluia.

IVY, CHIEF OF TREES.

This is also from the same manuscript as the foregoing.

  Ivy, chief of trees it is,
  Veni coronaberis.

HE most worthy she is in town,
 He that saith other doth amiss;
And worthy to bear the crown;
 Veni coronaberis.

Ivy is soft and meek of speech,
 Against all bale she is bliss;
Well is he that may her reach,
 Veni coronaberis.

Ivy is green with colour bright,
 Of all trees best she is;
And that I prove well now be right,
 Veni coronaberis.

[1] a large basket.

AND SONGS.

Ivy beareth berries black;
God grant us all His bliss,
For there shall we nothing lack:
Veni coronaberis.

THE CONTEST OF THE IVY AND THE HOLLY.

THIS is from a manuscript of Henry IV.'s time, in the British Museum. It appears that in 1561 W. Copeland paid the Company of Stationers 4*d.* for a license to print "A ballette entituled *holy and hyve.*" Brand, who has printed this carol in his "Observations on Popular Antiquities," says that from it "it should seem that holly was used only to deck the inside of houses at Christmas, while ivy was used not only as a vintner's sign, but also among the evergreens at funerals."

AY, Ivy, nay, it shall not be, I wis,
Let Holly have the mastery as the manner is.

Holly standeth in the hall fair to behold,
Ivy stands without the door; she is full sore a cold.
   Nay, Ivy, nay, &c.

Holly and his merry men, they dancen[1] and they sing;
Ivy and her maidens, they weepen[1] and they wring.
   Nay, Ivy, nay, &c.

Ivy hath a lybe,[2] she caught it with the cold,
So may they all have, that with Ivy hold.
   Nay, Ivy, nay, &c.

[1] The old form of the plural. [2] This word is not explained by any Glossary.

FESTIVE CAROLS

Holly hath berries, as red as any rose,
The foresters, the hunters, keep them from the does.
   Nay, Ivy, nay, &c.

Ivy hath berries as black as any sloe,
There come the owl and eat them as she go.
   Nay, Ivy, nay, &c.

Holly hath birds a full fair flock,
The nightingale, the poppinjay, the gentle laverock.
   Nay Ivy, nay, &c.

Good Ivy, [good Ivy,] what birds hast thou,
None but the owlet that cries How! How!
   Nay, Ivy, nay, &c.

A CHRISTMAS CAROL.

This curious specimen of an ancient drinking song is contained in a manuscript written early in the sixteenth century, and preserved in the Cottonian collection in the British Museum. It bears the title of "A Christenmesse Carroll."

 BONE, God wot!
 Sticks in my throat—
Without I have a draught
 Of cornie ale,
Nappy and stale,
My life lies in great waste.
Some ale or beer,

Gentle butler,
Some liquor thou us show,
  Such as you mash
  Our throats to wash,
The best ware that you brew.

  Saint, master, and knight,
  That Saint Malt hight,
Were pressed between two stones;
  That sweet humour
  Of his liquor
Would make us sing at once.
  Master Wortley,
  I dare well say,
I tell you as I think,
  Would not, I say,
  Bid us this day,
But that we should have drink.

  His men so tall
  Walk up his hall,
With many a comely dish;
  Of his good meat
  I cannot eat,
Without I drink, I wis.
  Now give us drink,
  And let cat wink,
I tell you all at once,
  It sticks so sore,
  I may sing no more,
Till I have drunken once.

A CHRISTMAS CAROL.

THIS singular carol is derived (through the medium of the "Bibliographical Miscellanies" of the late Dr. Bliss,) from the collection of Christmas Carols printed by Richard Kele about 1550. It is probably the earliest of a class of pieces which were in great favour a century or so afterwards; and many specimens of which may be seen in Percy's "Reliques of Ancient English Poetry," and Ritson's "Ancient Songs and Ballads," under the denomination of "Mad Songs;" in which the incoherent utterances of a maniac are made the vehicle of amusement. The present is the only instance of such a production being found in a collection of carols, although none can doubt the power of such a disconnected rhapsody to excite the boisterous merriment of a group of Christmas revellers, forgetful of all care and reflection, and bent only on amusement. The reader will observe the introduction into this carol of a device for raising a laugh frequently resorted to by modern *farceurs*, viz. the interchanging the positions of two of the words in a sentence; in this instance the words *cow* and *rope* in the line

"The cow brake loose, the rope ran home."

The allusions to the Canterbury Pilgrimage and St. Katherine of Kent show the carol to be of much earlier date than the time of publication. It is believed that it has never been reproduced (except by Dr. Bliss) since its original production.

Y heart of gold as true as steel,
    As I me leaned on a bough;
In faith but if ye love me well,
    Lord so Robin lough.[1]

[1] laughed.

FESTIVE CAROLS AND SONGS.

My lady went to Canterbury
    The Saint to be her boot;[1]
She met with Kate of Malmsbury
    Why shepyst[2] thou in a apple root?
           My heart, &c.

Nine mile to Michaelmas,
    Our dame began to brew,
Michael set his mare to grass,
    Lord so fast it snew.[3]
           My heart, &c.

For you, love, I brake my glass,
    Your gown is furred with blue;
The devil is dead: for there I was,
    I wis it is full true.
           My heart, &c.

And if ye sleep the cock will crow,
    True heart, think what I say,
Jack-a-napes will make a mow,[4]
    Look, who dare say him nay?
           My heart, &c.

I pray you have me now in mind,
    I tell you of the matter,

[1] help.   [2] hidest.   [3] snowed.   [4] mock.

He blew his horn against the wind;
    The crow goeth to the water.
              My heart, &c.

Yet I tell you mickle more,
    The cat lieth in the cradle,
I pray you keep true heart in store,
    A penny for a ladle.
              My heart, &c.

I swear by St. Katherine of Kent,
    The goose goeth to the green,
All our dog's tail is brent,[1]
    It is not as I ween.[2]
              My heart, &c.

Tyrlery lorpyn the laverock sung,
    So merrily pipes the sparrow:
The cow brake loose, the rope ran home,
    Sir, God give you good morrow.
              My heart, &c.

[1] burnt.   [2] guess.

A CHRISTMAS CAROL.

This brief effusion was printed by Ritson in his "Ancient Songs and Ballads." It is placed third in the class of pieces produced during the reigns of the four Stuart kings, whence we may presume that Ritson conceived it to belong to the period of either James or Charles I. The source from which it was obtained is not stated. It may possibly be a short salutation sung by the waits at the conclusion of their nocturnal instrumental performance to the occupants of the house before which they were playing.

OD bless the master of this house,
  The mistress also,
  And all the little children
   That round the table go :

And all your kin and kinsfolk
 That dwell both far and near ;
I wish you a merry Christmas,
 And a happy New Year.

A CHRISTMAS CAROL.

This excellent and sprightly carol is from the pen of George Wither, and first appeared, under the above title, in "A Miscelany of Epigrams, Sonnets, Epitaphs, and such other Verses" printed at the end of his poem called "Faire Virtve, the Mistresse of Philarete," in 1622. No better or livelier picture of the manner in which Christmas was celebrated in England before Puritanism became predominant can be presented to the reader.

    O, now is come our joyful'st feast;
      Let every man be jolly;
    Each room with ivy leaves is drest,
      And every post with holly.
        Though some churls at our mirth repine,
        Round your foreheads garlands twine,
        Drown sorrow in a cup of wine,
    And let us all be merry.

    Now, all our neighbours' chimneys smoke,
      And Christmas blocks are burning;
    Their ovens they with baked meats choke,
      And all their spits are turning.
        Without the door let sorrow lie;
        And if for cold it hap to die,
        We'll bury't it in a Christmas pie,
    And evermore be merry.

FESTIVE CAROLS.

Now every lad is wondrous trim,
    And no man minds his labour,
Our lasses have provided them
    A bag-pipe and a tabor;
        Young men and maids, and girls and boys,
        Give life to one another's joys;
        And you anon shall by their noise
Perceive that they are merry.

Rank misers now do sparing shun;
    Their hall of music soundeth;
And dogs thence with whole shoulders run,
    So all things there aboundeth.
        The country-folk themselves advance;
        For Crowdy-muttons[1] come out of France;
        And Jack shall pipe, and Jill shall dance,
And all the town be merry.

Ned Squash hath fetched his bands from pawn,
    And all his best apparel;
Brisk Nell hath bought a ruff of lawn
    With droppings of the barrel;[2]

---

[1] A by-word for a fiddler, derived from the crowth or crowd, a precursor of the violin.

[2] One of the verses of a contemporary ballad, called "Mock-beggar's Hall," commences with nearly the same words, viz:—

    "Ned Swash hath fetched his cloths from pawn,
        With dropping of the barrell;
    Joan Dust hath bought a smock of lawn,
        And now begins to quarrell."

FESTIVE CAROLS

    And those that hardly all the year
    Had bread to eat, or rags to wear,
    Will have both clothes and dainty fare,
And all the day be merry.

Now poor men to the justices
    With capons make their errants;
And if they hap to fail of these,
    They plague them with their warrants;[1]
        But now they feed them with good cheer,
        And what they want they take in beer;
        For Christmas comes but once a year,
And then they shall be merry.

Good farmers in the country nurse
    The poor, that else were undone;
Some landlords spend their money worse,
    On lust and pride at London.
        There, the roysters they do play,
        Drab and dice their lands away,
        Which may be ours another day;
And therefore let's be merry.

The client now his suit forbears,
    The prisoner's heart is eased;

---

[1] We need not be surprised that petty justices were guilty of such obliquity when we remember that about the period at which this carol was written the venality of judges was not unfrequent, even the great Bacon having stooped to "contaminate his fingers with base bribes."

AND SONGS.

The debtor drinks away his cares,
    And for the time is pleased.
        Though other purses be more fat,
            Why should we pine or grieve at that?
        Hang sorrow! care will kill a cat,
And therefore let's be merry.

Hark! how the wags abroad do call
    Each other forth to rambling:
Anon you'll see them in the hall
    For nuts and apples scrambling.
        Hark! how the roofs with laughter sound!
        Anon they'll think the house goes round;
        For they the cellar's depth have found,
And there they will be merry.

The wenches with their wassail bowls
    About the streets are singing;
The boys are come to catch the owls,[1]
    The wild mare in is bringing.[2]

---

[1] Brand, writing in 1795, says, "A credible person born and brought up in a village not far from Bury St. Edmunds, in the county of Suffolk, informed me that, when he was a boy, there was a rural custom there among the youths of *hunting owls and squirrels* on Christmas Day."

[2] No information can be gained of the nature of this sport. Herrick, in his *Hesperides*, mentions amongst other Christmas games,
                  "the care
      That young men have *to shoe the mare;*"
which may possibly have been the same diversion as that named in our carol.

FESTIVE CAROLS.

  Our kitchen-boy hath broke his box,[1]
   And to the dealing of the ox
   Our honest neighbours come by flocks,
  And here they will be merry.

  Now kings and queens poor sheep-cotes have,
   And mate with everybody;
  The honest now may play the knave,
   And wise men play at noddy,
    Some youths will now a mumming go,
    Some others play at Rowland-ho,[2]
    And twenty other gameboys[3] mo,
  Because they will be merry.

  Then wherefore in these merry days
   Should we, I pray, be duller?
  No, let us sing some roundelays,
   To make our mirth the fuller.
    And, whilest thus inspir'd we sing,
    Let all the streets with echoes ring,
    Woods and hills, and everything,
  Bear witness we are merry.

---

[1] The old Christmas money-box was made of earthenware, and required to be broken in order to get at the money it contained.

[2] This is also a sport which has slipped out of remembrance. It was possibly another name for hide-and-seek.

[3] From the Anglo-Norman *gambaudes*; gambols or pranks.

THE WASSAIL.

"Was-haile," and "Drink-heil" were the usual phrases of quaffing amongst the Anglo-Saxons, and were equivalent to the modern expressions "Good health," and "I drink to you." The custom of young women going about on New-year's Eve from house to house with a wassail bowl containing a composition of ale, nutmeg, sugar, toast, and roasted crab apples (sometimes called Lambs-wool) prevailed for ages. The bearers presented the bowl to the inmates of the houses where they called, sang some verses, and received in return a small gratuity. Selden, in his Table-talk, has made this custom the subject of a curious comparison. "The Pope," he says, "in sending relicks to Princes, does as wenches do to their Wassels at New Year's tide—they present you with a cup, and you must drink of a slabby stuff, but the meaning is, you must give them money, ten times more than it is worth." Prior to the suppression of the monasteries it was the custom for the wassail bowl to be placed on the Abbot's table and circulated amongst the community, under the title of *Poculum Caritatis*—the Cup of Charity, or Love. This custom is still preserved amongst us, and the very name retained, in the Loving Cup of civic banquets, and the Grace Cup of the universities. The Wassail song here presented is the production of Robert Herrick,— "the jovial Herrick" as the late Douglas Jerrold aptly named him—and appears to describe the visit of a set of Wassailers to the house of some person who refused them admission.

IVE way, give way, ye gates, and win
An easy blessing to your bin
And basket, by our entering in.

FESTIVE CAROLS

May both with manchet¹ stand replete,
Your larder, too, so hung with meat,
That though a thousand thousand eat,

Yet, ere twelve moons shall whirl about
Their silv'ry spheres, there's none may doubt
But more's sent in than was served out.

Next, may your dairies prosper so,
As that your pans no ebb may know;
But if they do, the more to flow:

Like to a solemn sober stream,
Bauked all with lilies; and the cream
Of sweetest cowslips filling them.

Then may your plants be pressed with fruit,
Nor bee, or hive you have be mute,
But sweetly sounding like a lute.

Next, may your duck and teeming hen,
Both to the cock's tread say, amen;
And for their two eggs render ten.

Last, may your harrows, shares, and ploughs,
Your stacks, your stocks, your sweetest mows,
All prosper by your virgin-vows.

---

¹ A small loaf of fine wheaten bread. The founder of the Hospital of St. Cross, near Winchester, directed that every stranger calling should receive a *manchet* of bread and a cup of ale; a custom which is, it is believed, still kept up.

Alas! we bless; but see none here,
That brings us either ale or beer;
In a dry house all things are near.

Let's leave a longer time to wait,
Where rust and cobwebs bind the gate,
And all live here with needy fate;

Where chimneys do for ever weep
For want of warmth, and stomachs keep
With noise the servants' eyes from sleep.

It is in vain to sing, or stay
Our free feet here, but we'll away,
Yet to the Larès this we'll say:

"The time will come, when you'll be sad,
And reckon this for fortune bad,
T' have lost the good ye might have had."

A MERRY CHRISTMAS CAROL.

THIS carol originally appeared in a collection of "Good and true, fresh and new, Christmas Carols," printed in black letter "by E. P. for Francis Coles, dwelling in the Old Bailey," in the year 1642, a copy of which is preserved amongst the books of Anthony à Wood, the antiquary, in the Ashmolean Museum, Oxford.

ALL you that are good fellows,
    Come hearken to my song;
I know you do not hate good cheer,
    Nor liquor that is strong.

FESTIVE CAROLS

I hope there is none here
    But soon will take my part,
Seeing my master and my dame
    Say welcome with their heart.

This is a time of joyfulness
    And merry time of year,
When as the rich with plenty stor'd
    Do make the poor good cheer.
Plum porridge, roast beef, and mince pies
    Stand smoking on the board,
With other brave varieties
    Our master doth afford.

Our mistress and her cleanly maids
    Have neatly play'd the cooks;
Methinks these dishes eagerly
    At my sharp stomach looks,
As though they were afraid
    To see me draw my blade;
But I reveng'd on them will be
    Until my stomach's stay'd.

Come fill us of the strongest,
    Small drink is out of date;
Methinks I shall fare like a prince
    And sit in gallant state.
This is no miser's feast,
    Although that things be dear;
God grant the founder of this feast
    Each Christmas keep good cheer.

AND SONGS.

This day for Christ we celebrate,
   Who was born at this time;
For which all Christians should rejoice
   And I do sing in rhyme.
When you have given thanks
   Unto your dainties fall;
Heav'n bless my master and my dame,
   Lord bless me and you all.

A CAROL FOR THE WASSAIL BOWL.

THIS carol is from an undated black-letter collection, called "New Christmas Carrols: Being fit also to be sung at Easter, Whitsontide, and other Festival days in the year," preserved amongst the books of Anthony à Wood, in the Ashmolean Museum. It bears the title of "A Carrol for a Wassel Bowl to be sung upon Twelfth Day at night—to the tune of *Gallants, come away.*" The custom of bringing in a wassail bowl on Twelfth Night was used in the time of Henry VII, and amongst the Ordinances for his household during Christmas, the following occurs in reference to Twelfth Night:—"Item, the chappell to stand on one side of the Hall, and when the Steward cometh in at the Hall-dore with the Wassell, he must crie three tymes, *Wassell, Wassell, Wassell*; and then the chappell to answere with a good song."

 JOLLY Wassail-bowl,
   A Wassail of good ale,
   Well fare the butler's soul,
   That setteth this to sale;
      Our jolly Wassail.

FESTIVE CAROLS

Good dame, here at your door,
  Our Wassail we begin,
We are all maidens poor,
  We now pray let us in
      With our Wassail.

Our Wassail we do fill
  With apples and with spice,
Then grant us your good will,
  To taste here once or twice
      Of our Wassail.

If any maidens be
  Here dwelling in this house,
They kindly will agree
  To take a full carouse
      Of our Wassail.

But here they let us stand
  All freezing in the cold;
Good master, give command
  To enter and be bold,
      With our Wassail.

Much joy into this hall
  With us is entered in,
Our master first of all,
  We hope will now begin
      Of our Wassail.

AND SONGS.

And after, his good wife
  Our spiced bowl will try,—
The Lord prolong your life!
  Good fortune we espy
      For our Wassail.

Some bounty from your hands,
  Our Wassail to maintain:
We'll buy no house nor lands
  With that which we do gain
      With our Wassail.

This is our merry night
  Of choosing King and Queen,
Then be it your delight
  That something may be seen
      In our Wassail.

It is a noble part
  To bear a liberal mind;
God bless our master's heart!
  For here we comfort find
      With our Wassail.

And now we must be gone,
  To seek out more good cheer;
Where bounty will be shown,
  As we have found it here,
      With our Wassail.

FESTIVE CAROLS

Much joy betide them all,
Our prayers shall be still,
We hope, and ever shall,
For this your great good will
To our Wassail.

GLOUCESTERSHIRE WASSAILERS' CAROL.

THIS carol was seventy years since communicated by Samuel Lysons to Brand, with the information that it was then still sung in Gloucestershire, and that the Wassailers brought with them a great bowl dressed up with garlands and ribbon. The names of the horse, mare, and cow in this copy—Dobbin, Smiler, and Fillpail—are left blank in Brand's copy, to be supplied by the singers as circumstances required. Persons still living remember the Wassailers singing this carol from house to house in some of the villages by the Severn side below Gloucester, nearly fifty years since, and the custom has been uninterruptedly maintained and still subsists in the western parts of the county. On New Year's Eve, December 31st, 1864, the carol was sung in the little village of Over, near Gloucester, by a troop of Wassailers from the neighbouring village of Minsterworth.

ASSAIL! Wassail! all over the town,
Our toast it is white, our ale it is brown;
Our bowl it is made of a maplin tree,
We be good fellows all—I drink to thee.

Here's to Dobbin, and to his right ear,
God send our master a happy New Year;
A happy New Year as e'er he did see—
With my Wassailing Bowl I drink to thee.

AND SONGS.

Here's to Smiler, and to her right eye,
God send our mistress a good Christmas pie;
A good Christmas pie as e'er I did see—
With my Wassailing Bowl I drink to thee.

Here's to Fillpail, and to her long tail,
God send our master us never may fail
Of a cup of good beer; I pray you draw near,
And then you shall hear our jolly Wassail.

Be here any maids? I suppose there be some—
Sure they'll not let young men stand on the cold stone;
Sing hey, O maids, come troll back the pin,
And the fairest maid in the house let us all in.

Come, butler, come bring us a bowl of the best,
I hope your soul in heaven will rest;
But if you do bring us a bowl of the small,
Then down shall go butler, bowl, and all.

WASSAILERS' CAROL.

This carol is from a broadside printed at Bradford in Yorkshire within the last twenty years. Its appearance so recently seems to furnish presumptive evidence of the custom of Wassailing, or, at least, some remains of it, being still in existence in the West Riding of the great northern county. It seems also to have attained some popularity in the adjoining county of Lancaster, having been printed, under the title of a "Wessel Cup Hymn," in a chap-book printed at Manchester, called "A Selection of Christmas Hymns," whence it has been transferred to Mr. Harland's recently published volume of "The Ballads and Songs of Lancashire." Although the carol may in the main be of no great antiquity, it is observable that the penultimate verse is identical with the commencement of a short carol printed by Ritson as of the time of James or Charles I. Many single verses, or even shorter fragments of early compositions, have, there can be no doubt, been handed down by oral repetition, and eventually embodied in modern carols.

ERE we come a wassailing
    Among the leaves so green,
Here we come a wandering,
    So fair to be seen.

Chorus.
Love and joy come to you,
And to your wassail too,
And God send you a happy new year,
    A new year;
And God send you a happy new year.
Our wassail cup is made of the rosemary tree,
So is your beer of the best barley.

FESTIVE CAROLS.

We are not daily beggars,
    That beg from door to door,
But we are neighbours' children,
    Whom you have seen before.

Call up the butler of this house,
    Put on his golden ring,
Let him bring us up a glass of beer,
    And better we shall sing.

We have got a little purse
    Made of stretching leather skin,
We want a little of your money
    To line it well within.

Bring us out a table,
    And spread it with a cloth,
Bring us out a mouldy cheese,
    And some of your Christmas loaf.

God bless the master of this house,
    Likewise the mistress too;
And all the little children,
    That round the table go.

Good master and mistress,
    While you're sitting by the fire,
Pray think of us poor children,
    Who are wandering in the mire.

CHRISTMAS CUSTOMS.

The following series of short poems illustrative of old Christmas customs and superstitions is selected from the "Hesperides" of Robert Herrick, first published in 1648. Few writers have been so thoroughly conversant with the popular superstitions of their time, or have so pleasantly interwoven them into their poetry, as Herrick; hence his verses have a life-like character and a charm which leads captive every reader.

I.

ON CHRISTMAS EVE.

On this eve our ancestors were wont to lay a log of wood upon the fire, called a Yule-clog, or log, or Christmas block, to illuminate the house. It was a custom to preserve a portion of this block until the next year, with which to light the new block, and the omission so to do was deemed unlucky. The practice still prevails in many parts of the country.

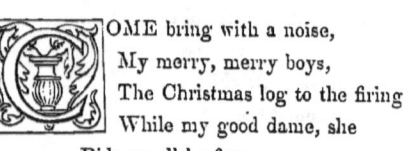

COME bring with a noise,
   My merry, merry boys,
The Christmas log to the firing;
   While my good dame, she
  Bids ye all be free,
And drink to your heart's desiring.

  With the last year's brand
  Light the new block, and
For good success in his spending,

FESTIVE CAROLS.

On your psalteries play,
That sweet luck may
Come while the log is a teending.[1]

Drink now the strong beer,
Cut the white loaf here,
The while the meat is a shredding
For the rare mince-pie,
And the plums standing by,
To fill the paste that's a kneading.

II.

ON CHRISTMAS EVE.

ANOTHER CEREMONY.

THE Christmas pie alluded to in these lines was not, as many might suppose, a mince-pie—such a Christmas pie as Little Jack Horner sat eating in his corner—but a much more elaborate and extensive compound of good things in use amongst our forefathers in olden times. The records of the Worshipful Company of Salters of London contain a receipt written in 1394, in the reign of Richard II, instructing the cooks of that age how "For to make a moost choyce paaste of gamys to be eaten at y*e* feste of Chrystemasse," a copy of which, in modern spelling, is here presented for the delectation of the reader.

"*For to make a most choice pasty of game to be eaten at the Feast of Christmas.*

"Take Pheasant, Hare, and Chicken, or Capon, of each one; with two Partridges, two Pigeons, and two Conies; and smite them in pieces, and pick clean away therefrom all the bones that ye may, and therewith do them into a foyle[2] of good paste, made craftily in the likeness of a bird's body, with the livers and hearts, two kidneys of sheep, and forces[3]

[1] kindling.   [2] crust.   [3] forced-meat.

FESTIVE CAROLS

and eyren[1] made into balls. Cast thereto powder of pepper, salt, spice, eysell[2] and fungus[3] pickled; and then take the bones and let them seethe in a pot to make a good broth therefor, and do it into the foyle of paste, and close it up fast and bake it well, and so serve it forth, with the head of one of the birds stuck at one end of the foyle and a great tail at the other, and divers of his long feathers set in cunningly all about him."

Christmas pies of large dimensions, prepared somewhat in the same way, continue to be made in some parts of Yorkshire, and from their use being principally confined to that county are commonly called "Yorkshire pies."

This custom of sitting up to preserve the Christmas pie from depredators is not mentioned elsewhere than in these lines.

OME, guard this night the Christmas pie,
That the thief, though ne'er so sly,
With his flesh-hooks don't come nigh
  To catch it
From him who all alone sits there,
Having his eyes still in his ear,
And a deal of nightly fear,
  To watch it.

III.

TWELFTH NIGHT;

OR, KING AND QUEEN.

THE Twelfth Cake was formerly made full of plums, amongst which were placed a bean and a pea. The cake being cut into slices and distributed amongst the company, he to whose lot fell the piece containing the bean was called King, whilst she who obtained the piece holding the pea became Queen, for the evening. This ceremony was also formerly practised in France, under the name of "La Roi de la Fève."

[1] eggs.   [2] vinegar.   [3] mushrooms.

OW, now, the mirth comes,
  With the cake full of plums,
Where Bean's the king of the sport here;
  Besides we must know,
  The Pea also
Must revel, as queen, in the court here.

  Begin then to choose,
  This night as ye use,
Who shall for the present delight here,
  Be a king by the lot,
  And who shall not
Be Twelfth-day queen for the night here.

  Which known, let us make
  Joy-sops with the cake;
And let not a man then be seen here,
  Who, unurg'd, will not drink,
  To the base from the brink,
A health to the king and queen here.

  Next crown the bowl full
  With the gentle lamb's-wool,[1]
Add sugar, nutmeg, and ginger,
  With store of ale too;
  And thus ye must do
To make the wassail a swinger.

[1] A compound of strong beer, roasted apples, sugar and spice.

FESTIVE CAROLS.

Give then to the king
And queen wassailing;
And, though with ale ye be wet here,
Yet part ye from hence
As free from offence,
As when ye innocent met here.

IV.

SAINT DISTAFF'S DAY;

OR, THE MORROW AFTER TWELFTH-DAY.

It is scarcely necessary to observe that the name of St. Distaff will not be found in the calendar. The name was applied to this day as being that on which, as the first after the Christmas holidays, the women resumed the distaff and recommenced their usual employment. As, after a cessation from work, people are sometimes reluctant either to resume it themselves, or to allow others to do so, so it appears to have been customary on this day for the indolent amongst the men to set fire to the flax and tow of the more industrious of the fair sex, in retaliation for which the damsels brought pails of water and threw over the men.

ARTLY work and partly play
Ye must, on St. Distaff's day;
From the plough soon free your team,
Then come home and fodder them;
If the maids a spinning go,
Burn the flax and fire the tow.
Bring in pails of water then,
Let the maids bewash the men.

AND SONGS.

Give St. Distaff all the right,
Then bid Christmas sport good night,
And next morrow every one
To his own vocation.

V.

CANDLEMAS EVE.

On this day the Christmas ceremonies, which had lingered on after Twelfth-day, finally closed, and all traces of them were removed. The custom long prevailed, and there must be many still living who can remember the evergreens with which our churches were decorated at Christmas, remaining until Candlemas.

OWN with the rosemary, and so
Down with the bays and mistletoe;
Down with the holly, ivy, all
Wherewith ye deck'd the Christmas hall;
That so the superstitious find
No one least branch there left behind:
For look! how many leaves there be
Neglected there, Maids, trust to me,
So many goblins you shall see.

VI.

CANDLEMAS EVE.

OWN with the rosemary and bays,
    Down with the mistletoe;
Instead of holly now upraise
    The greener box for show.

The holly hitherto did sway,
    Let box now domineer,
Until the dancing Easter day,
    Or Easter's Eve appear.

Then youthful box which now hath grace
    Your houses to renew,
Grown old, surrender must his place
    Unto the crisped yew.

When yew is out, then birch comes in,
    And many flowers beside,
Both of a fresh and fragrant kin,
    To honour Whitsuntide.

Green rushes then, and sweetest bents,
    With cooler oaken boughs,
Come in for comely ornaments,
    To readorn the house.

Thus times do shift; each thing his turn does hold;
New things succeed as former things grow old.

AND SONGS.

VII.

CANDLEMAS DAY.

THE custom noticed in the first of these extracts is here again more particularly mentioned, and a reason for its observance given.

INDLE the Christmas brand, and then
Till sunset let it burn;
Which quench'd then lay it up again
Till Christmas next return.

Part must be kept wherewith to teend
The Christmas log next year;
And where 'tis safely kept, the fiend
Can do no mischief there.

CHRISTMAS'S LAMENTATION.

THIS piece, having more of the character of a ballad than of a carol, may possibly be considered as rather out of place in the present collection; but its singularity, its curious exhibition of the decay of hospitality and general degeneracy of the times, and its striking contrast with the following carol, which is a kind of reply to it, seemed to call for its insertion. It is found on a very rare, and perhaps unique, broadsheet, preserved in the very valuable collection known as the Roxburgh Ballads, in the British Museum. The full title is "Christmas' Lamentation for the losse of his acquaintance; showing how he is forst to leave the Country and come to London. To the tune of *Now the Spring is come.* Printed at London for F[rancis] C[oles] dwelling in the old Bayly."

FESTIVE CAROLS

The mention of "yellow starch" as a fashionable frivolity shows the date of the production of the ballad to be between the latter end of Elizabeth's reign and the close of the year 1615, when "yellow starch" grew into disfavour in consequence, it is said, of Anne Turner, one of the accomplices of King James and the Somersets in the murder of Sir Thomas Overbury, and the introducer of the fashion, appearing at the place of execution, pursuant to her sentence, in "a cobweb lawn ruff of that colour;"—and, what must have appeared more odious still in the eyes of "the fashionable world," the hangman being tricked out for the occasion with "bands and cuffs of yellow."

Repetitions of words, similar to those forming the second and fifth lines of the first verse, occur in every verse of the original; but as these are only occasioned by the exigencies of the tune to which the ballad is to be sung, it has been thought advisable to omit them in the present copy.

HRISTMAS is my name, far have I gone,
Have I gone, have I gone, have I gone,
  without regard,
Whereas great men by flocks there be flown,
There be flown, there be flown, there be flown,
  to London-ward;
Where they in pomp and pleasure do waste
That which Christmas was wonted to feast,
  Welladay!
Houses where music was wont for to ring
Nothing but bats and owlets do sing.
 Welladay! Welladay! Welladay!
  where should I stay?

Christmas beef and bread is turn'd into stones
  and silken rags;
And Lady Money sleeps and makes moans
  in misers' bags:

AND SONGS.

Houses where pleasure once did abound,
Nought but a dog and a shepherd is found,
    Welladay!
Places where Christmas revels did keep
Are now become habitations for sheep.
   Welladay! Welladay! Welladay!
    where should I stay?

Pan, the shepherd's god, doth deface
    Lady Ceres' crown,
And tillage that doth go to decay
    in every town:
Landlords their rents so highly enhance
That Pierce, the ploughman, bare-foot may dance;
    Welladay!
And farmers that Christmas would entertain,
Have scarce wherewith themselves to maintain.
   Welladay! Welladay! Welladay!
    where should I stay?

Come to the countryman, he will protest,
    and of bull beef boast;
And for the citizen, he is so hot
    he will burn the roast.
The courtier he good deeds will not scorn,
Nor will he see poor Christmas forlorn:
    Welladay!
Since none of these good deeds will do,
Christmas had best turn courtier too.
   Welladay! Welladay! Welladay
    where should I stay?

FESTIVE CAROLS

Pride and luxury they do devour
    housekeeping quite;
And beggary that doth beget
    in many a knight.
Madam, forsooth, in her coach must wheel,
Although she wear her hose out at heel,
    Welladay!
And on her back wear that for a weed
Which me and all my fellows would feed.
  Welladay! Welladay! Welladay!
    where should I stay?

Since pride came up with the yellow starch,
    poor folks do want,
And nothing the rich men will to them give,
    but do them taunt;
For Charity from the country is fled,
And in her place hath left naught but need;
    Welladay!
And corn is grown to so high a price,
It makes poor men cry with weeping eyes.
  Welladay! Welladay! Welladay!
    where should I stay?

Briefly for to end, here I do find
    so great vacation,
That most great houses seem to attain
    a strong purgation:
Where purging pills such effects they have shown,
That forth of doors their owners have thrown,
    Welladay!

And whereas Christmas comes by and calls,
Nought but solitary and naked walls.
    Welladay! Welladay! Welladay!
      where shall I stay?

Philemon's cottage was turned into gold
    for harbouring Jove:
Rich men their houses for to keep
    might their greatness move;
But in the city they say they do live,
Where gold by handfuls away they do give:
    I'll away,
And thither therefore I purpose to pass,
Hoping at London to find the Golden Ass.
    I'll away, I'll away, I'll away,
      for here's no stay.

OLD CHRISTMAS RETURNED.

THIS lively carol, which is a kind of reply to the preceding, exists on a broadsheet preserved amongst the famous collection of ballads, &c. formed by Samuel Pepys, secretary to the Admiralty (whose diary has afforded us so much valuable information and so many an hour's amusement), and by him bequeathed to Magdalene College, Cambridge. The full title runs as follows:—

"Old Christmas returned, or Hospitality revived; being a Looking-glass for Rich Misers, wherein they may see (if they be not blind) how much they are to blame for their penurious house-keeping, and likewise

FESTIVE CAROLS

an encouragement to those noble-minded gentry, who lay out a great part of their estates in hospitality, relieving such persons as have need thereof:

"Who feasts the poor, a true reward shall find,
Or helps the old, the feeble, lame, and blind."

"Tune of the *Delights of the Botlle*."

There is scarcely any evil which is wholly unmixed with good, and there is much good which has its concomitant evil. Amongst the few good things which were intermingled with the many evils ensuing on the restoration to political power of the treacherous and depraved Stuarts, the return to the time-honoured custom of celebrating Christmas, both religiously and festively, was one of the most prominent; and it might be supposed, were we to trust to the internal evidence only, that this carol was written to welcome that event, either at the Christmas of 1660, or at the latest of that of 1661. But its being directed to be sung to the tune of a song in Matthew Locke's opera of "Psyche," which was not performed until 1675, shows it to have been written after that date, unless, indeed, we resort to the hypothesis of its having been originally sung to another tune, which became abandoned on account of the popularity of Locke's song.

The line at the commencement of the ninth verse is an allusion to a ballad very popular during the first half of the seventeenth century, entitled "Mock-beggar's Hall stands empty," which was levelled at the prevalent indulgence in external pomp and luxury, to provide the means for which the domestic comforts were much reduced and the old hospitality nearly abandoned. "Mock-beggar's Hall" was a name applied to a house having a well-looking exterior but a mean interior.

LL you that to feasting and mirth are inclined,
Come, here is good news for to pleasure your mind;
Old Christmas is come for to keep open house,
He scorns to be guilty of starving a mouse;
 Then come, boys, and welcome, for diet the chief,
 Plum-pudding, goose, capon, minc'd pies, and roast beef.

AND SONGS.

A long time together he hath been forgot,
They scarce could afford for to hang on the pot;
Such miserly sneaking in England hath been,
As by our forefathers ne'er used to be seen;
But, now he's return'd, you shall have in brief,
Plum-pudding, goose, capon, minc'd pies, and roast beef.

The times were ne'er good since old Christmas was fled,
And all hospitality hath been so dead,
No mirth at our festivals late did appear,
They scarcely would part with a cup of March beer;
But now you shall have, for the ease of your grief,
Plum-pudding, goose, capon, minc'd pies, and roast beef.

The butler and baker they now may be glad,
The times they are mended, though they have been bad;
The brewer he likewise may be of good cheer,
He shall have good trading for ale and strong beer;
All trades shall be jolly, and have for relief,
Plum-pudding, goose, capon, minc'd pies, and roast beef.

The holly and ivy about the walls wind,
And show that we ought to our neighbours be kind,
Inviting each other for pastime and sport,
And where we best fare, there we most do resort;
We fail not for victuals, and that of the chief,
Plum-pudding, goose, capon, minc'd pies, and roast beef.

The cooks shall be busied, by day and by night,
In roasting and boiling, for taste and delight;
Their senses in liquor that's nappy they'll steep,

FESTIVE CAROLS

Though they be afforded to have little sleep;
They still are employed for to dress us, in brief,
Plum-pudding, goose, capon, minc'd pies, and roast beef.

Although the cold weather doth hunger provoke,
'Tis a comfort to see how the chimneys do smoke;
Provision is making for beer, ale, and wine,
For all that are willing or ready to dine;
Then haste to the kitchen for diet the chief,
Plum-pudding, goose, capon, minc'd pies, and roast beef.

All travellers, as they do pass on their way,
At gentlemen's halls are invited to stay,
Themselves to refresh, and their horses to rest,
Since that he must be Old Christmas's guest;
Nay, the poor shall not want, but have for relief,
Plum-pudding, goose, capon, minc'd pies, and roast beef.

Now Mock-beggar Hall it no more shall stand empty,
But all shall be furnished with freedom and plenty;
The hoarding old misers, who used to preserve
The gold in their coffers, and see the poor starve,
Must now spread their tables, and give them, in brief,
Plum-pudding, goose, capon, minc'd pies, and roast beef.

The court, and the city, and country are glad;
Old Christmas is come to cheer up the sad;
Broad pieces and guineas about now shall fly,
And hundreds be losers by cogging a die;
Whilst others are feasting with diet the chief,
Plum-pudding, goose, capon, minc'd pies, and roast beef.

AND SONGS.

Those that have no coin at the cards for to play,
May sit by the fire and pass time away,
And drink of their moisture contented and free;
"My honest good fellow, come here is to thee!"
And when they are hungry, fall to their relief,
Plum-pudding, goose, capon, minc'd pies, and roast beef.

Young gallants and ladies shall foot it along,
Each room in the house to the music shall throng,
Whilst jolly carouses about they shall pass,
And each country swain trip about with his lass;
Meantime goes the caterer to fetch in the chief,
Plum-pudding, goose, capon, minc'd pies, and roast beef.

The cooks and the scullion who toil in their frocks,
Their hopes do depend upon their Christmas-box;
There are very few that do live on the earth
But enjoy at this time either profit or mirth;
Yea, those that are charged to find all relief,
Plum-pudding, goose, capon, minc'd pies, and roast beef.

Then well may we welcome Old Christmas to town,
Who brings us good cheer and liquor so brown,
To pass the cold winter away with delight,
We feast it all day, and we frolic all night;
Both hunger and cold we keep out with relief,
Plum-pudding, goose, capon, minc'd pies, and roast beef.

Then let all curmudgeons, who dote on their wealth,
And value their treasure much more than their health,

FESTIVE CAROLS

Go hang themselves up, if they will be so kind,
Old Christmas with them but small welcome shall find:
They will not afford to themselves, without grief,
Plum-pudding, goose, capon, minc'd pies, and roast beef.

A CHRISTMAS CAROL.

This is from " New Carolls for this Mery Time of Christmas," published in 1661, where it is directed to be sung to the tune of " Essex's last Good Night," a ballad written on the untimely fate of Queen Elizabeth's favourite. The last two verses bear some resemblance to the concluding verse of an old carol of an exceedingly mediocre kind, on St. John the Baptist's day, viz :—

> " Now kindly for my pretty song,
> Good butler, draw some beer;
> You know what dainties do belong
> To him that sings so clear.
> Holly and ivy to drink will drive ye
> To the brown bowl of perry;
> Apples and ale, with Christmas tale,
> Will make a household merry."

ALL you that in this house be here,
Remember Christ that for us died,
And spend away with modest cheer
In loving sort this Christmas tide.

And, whereas plenty God hath sent,
Give frankly to your friends in love:
The bounteous mind is freely bent,
And never will a niggard prove.

AND SONGS.

Our table spread within the hall,
    I know a banquet is at hand,
And friendly sort to welcome all
    That will unto their tacklings stand.

The maids are bonny girls, I see,
    Who have provided much good cheer,
Which, at my dame's commandment, be
    Now set upon the table here.

For I have here two knives in store,
    To lend to him that wanteth one;
Commend my wits, good lads, therefore,
    That come now hither having none.

For, if I should, no Christmas pie
    Would fall, I doubt, unto my share;
Wherefore, I will my manhood try,
    To fight a battle if I dare.

For pastry-crust, like castle walls,
    Stands braving me unto my face;
I am not well until it falls,
    And I made captain of the place.

The prunes, so lovely, look on me,
    I cannot choose but venture on:
The pie-meat spiced brave I see,
    The which I must not let alone.

FESTIVE CAROLS

Then, butler, fill me forth some beer,
  My song hath made me somewhat dry;
And so again to this good cheer,
  I'll quickly fall courageously.

And for my master I will pray,
  With all that of his household are,
Both old and young, that long we may
  Of God's good blessings have a share.

A CHRISTMAS SONG.

The old almanacks occasionally contained carols. The following is from "Poor Robin's Almanack" for 1695. This almanack enjoyed a long continuance of public favour, having appeared regularly from 1663 to 1828. The earlier numbers were said to have been written by Robert Herrick, the poet, from whom also the almanack was supposed to have derived its name. As regards the last particular, however, Antony à Wood gives a different account, viz. that the name was given in derision of Robert Pory, D.D., a noted pluralist, and that a mock "Imprimatur" purporting to bear his signature was placed on the title of the first number. The following lively and genial effusion has somewhat of a spice of Herrick's quality, although it is not at all likely to be of his production, as he died, at a very advanced age, several years before its publication. It is here given from Brand's "Observations on Popular Antiquities," as it has not been found possible to meet with a copy of the almanack for 1695. There appears to have been an additional verse concluding the carol, but of which Brand has perserved the last four lines only, viz:—

  "But as for curmudgeons
    Who will not be free,
  I wish they may die
    On the three-legged tree."

AND SONGS.

The "three-legged tree" was the erection at Tyburn on which malefactors suffered the extreme penalty of the law. It consisted of three horizontal beams joined together in the form of a triangle, and supported by three upright posts.

OW thrice welcome Christmas,
    Which brings us good cheer,
  Minc'd pies and plum-porridge,
    Good ale and strong beer;
With pig, goose, and capon,
    The best that can be,
So well doth the weather
    And our stomachs agree.

Observe how the chimnies
    Do smoke all about,
The cooks are providing
    For dinner, no doubt;
But those on whose tables
    No victuals appear,
O may they keep Lent
    All the rest of the year!

With holly and ivy
    So green and so gay;
We deck up our houses
    As fresh as the day,
With bays and rosemary
    And laurel complete,
And every one now
    Is a king in conceit.

A CHRISTMAS CAROL.

This is from "Poor Robin's Almanack" for the year 1700.

NOW that the time is come wherein
    Our Saviour Christ was born,
    The larders full of beef and pork,
    The garners filled with corn;
As God hath plenty to thee sent,
    Take comfort of thy labours,
And let it never thee repent
    To feast thy needy neighbours.

Let fires in every chimney be,
    That people they may warm them;
Tables with dishes covered,
    Good victuals will not harm them.
With mutton, veal, beef, pig, and pork,
    Well furnish every board,
Plum-pudding, furmity, and what
    Thy stock will then afford.

No niggard of the liquor be,
    Let it go round thy table;
People may freely drink, but not
    So long as they are able.

FESTIVE CAROLS.

Good customs they may be abused,
  Which makes rich men so slack us,
This feast is to relieve the poor,
  And not to drunken Bacchus.

Thus if thou doest,
  T'will credit raise thee;
God will thee bless,
  And neighbours praise thee.

THE APPROACH OF CHRISTMAS.

This carol, which is occasionally found elsewhere, under the title of "A Hint to the Fanaticks," originally appeared in "Poor Robin's Almanack" for 1711.

OW Christmas Day approaches near,
  Trim up the house with holly,
And set abroach the strongest beer,
  For neighbours to be jolly.
Let fanatics old customs blame,
  Yet Christmas is a High day,
Though they will fast upon the same,
  And feast upon Good Friday.

Good works are popishly inclined,
  Say they that none will do,
Yet they for pride can money find,
  And keep a coach also.

FESTIVE CAROLS

Thus, that which should relieve the poor,
    And feast them at this tide,
Is spent upon a coach and four,
    To maintain foolish pride.

Yet some there are, although but few,
    In whom more goodness lurks,
Who, to the poor will pity show,
    And show their faith by works.
I wish, for one, that these were twain,
    And knaves away all swept,
That honest Christmas once again
    With feasting may be kept.

CHRISTMAS CHEER.

THESE lines appeared in "Poor Robin's Almanack" for 1723. In the observations in the almanack on the month of December, the following remarks occur, which, as showing some of the customs of the period, are not undeserving of preservation. The writer, it will be observed, has not omitted the customary growl at the degeneracy of the age, although he has couched it under the milder form of the expression of a hope. "Now comes on old merry plentiful Christmas. The Husbandman lays his great Log behind the fire, and with a few of his neighbours over a good fire, taps his Christmas beer, cuts his Christmas cheese, and sets forward for a merry Christmas. The Landlord (for we hope there are yet some generous ones left) invites his Tenants and Labourers, and

AND SONGS.

with a good Sirloin of Roast Beef, and a few pitchers of nappy ale or beer, he wisheth them all a merry Christmas. The beggar begs his bread, sells some of it for money to buy drink, and without fear of being arrested, or call'd upon for parish duties, has as merry a Christmas as any of them all."

OW Christmas time is coming on,
  And, painful Harvest past and gone;
  Now reap the fruit of all your care
  With Christmas pies and good strong beer,
Sirloins of beef and hams of bacon,
With hollow meats,[1] roast goose and capon;
With good strong liquor; but take care
To let the poor come in for share.

Now hey for Christmas, let the spits go round,
Let cauldrons boil and pies i' th' oven be found.
May they who now deny themselves good cheer,
Against their wills keep strict Lent all the year.

[1] poultry, rabbits, &c.

A CHRISTMAS SONG.

This song is from a very curious and uncommon little book, entitled "Round About our Coal Fire, or Christmas Entertainments;" which treats not only of "the Mirth and Jollity of the Christmas Holidays; viz: Christmas Gambols, Eating, Drinking, Kissing, and other Diversions;" but of a variety of other things, such as Hobgoblins, Ghosts, Witches, Fairies, Jack the Giant-killer, and (that never-ceasing complaint) the Decay of Hospitality. The fourth edition of this work (the earliest known) appeared in 1734. The song here given serves as a "Prologue" to the book. The tune named in the last verse but one is that of a country dance which enjoyed a lengthened career of popularity. That amusing gossip, Pepys, mentions it in his account of a Court ball at which he was present on New Year's Eve, 1662. "Mr. Povy and I to White Hall; he taking me thither on purpose to carry me into the ball this night before the King [Charles II.]. He brought me first to the Duke's chamber, where I saw him and the Duchesse at supper; and thence into the room where the ball was to be, crammed with fine ladies, the greatest of the Court. By and by, comes the King and Queene, the Duke and Duchesse, and all the great ones: and after seating themselves, the King takes out the Duchesse of York; and the Duke the Duchesse of Buckingham; the Duke of Monmouth my Lady Castlemaine; and so other lords other ladies; and they danced the Brantle [Braule.] After that, the King led a lady a single Coranto; and then the rest of the lords, one after another, other ladies: very noble it was, and great pleasure to see. Then to country dances; the King leading the first, which he called for; *which was, says he, 'Cuckolds all awry,' the old dance of England.*" The tune may be seen in Mr. Chappell's excellent work, "Popular Music of the Olden Time."

FESTIVE CAROLS.

YOU merry, merry souls,
　　Christmas is a coming;
We shall have flowing bowls,
　　Dancing, piping, drumming.

Delicate minced pies,
　　To feast every virgin,
Capon and goose likewise,
　　Brawn, and a dish of sturgeon.

Then for your Christmas-box
　　Sweet plum cakes and money,
Delicate Holland smocks,
　　Kisses sweet as honey.

Hey for the Christmas ball,
　　Where we shall be jolly;
Coupling short and tall,
　　Kate, Dick, Ralph, and Molly.

Then to the hop we'll go,
　　Where we'll jig and caper
"Cuckolds all a-row;"
　　Will shall pay the scraper.

Hodge shall dance with Prue,
　　Keeping time with kisses;
We'll have a jovial crew
　　Of sweet smirking misses.

WELCOME, MERRY CHRISTMAS.

This very pleasing carol, in all probability one of the latest productions of its class, is from a broadside printed at Devonport, and intended for circulation throughout Devonshire, Cornwall, and Monmouthshire. It furnishes evidence of considerable ability in the unknown writer, and we might look in vain, perhaps, for a better exhortation to remembrance of the Psalmist's text, " Blessed is he that considereth the poor and needy; the Lord shall deliver him in the time of trouble."

E merry all, be merry all,
With holly dress the festive hall,
Prepare the song, the feast, the ball,
    To welcome merry Christmas.

And oh! remember, gentles gay,
For you who bask in fortune's ray,
The year is all a holiday,—
    The poor have only Christmas.

When you with velvets mantled o'er
Defy December's tempest's roar,
Oh, spare one garment from your store,
    To clothe the poor at Christmas.

When you the costly banquet deal
To guests, who never famine feel,
Oh, spare one morsel from your meal,
    To feed the poor at Christmas.

FESTIVE CAROLS.

When gen'rous wine your care controls,
And gives new joy to happiest souls,
Oh, spare one goblet from your bowls,
    To cheer the poor at Christmas.

So shall each note of mirth appear
More sweet to heaven than praise or prayer,
And Angels, in their Carols there,
    Shall bless the poor at Christmas.

THE TWELVE DAYS OF CHRISTMAS.

THIS piece is found on broadsides printed at Newcastle at various periods during the last hundred and fifty years. On one of these sheets, nearly a century old, it is entitled "An Old English Carol," but it can scarcely be said to fall within that description of composition, being rather fitted for use in playing the game of "Forfeits," to which purpose it was commonly applied in the metropolis upwards of forty years since. The practice was for one person in the company to recite the first three lines; a second, the four following; and so on; the person who failed in repeating her portion correctly being subjected to some trifling forfeit. The lady who was the favoured recipient of the gifts enumerated must have required no small extent of shelf or table room for their accommodation, as at the end of the Christmas festivities she must have found herself in possession of twelve partridges in pear trees, twenty-two turtle-doves, thirty French hens, thirty-six colley [i. e. black] birds, forty gold rings, forty-two laying geese, forty-two swimming swans, forty milk-maids, thirty-six drummers, thirty pipers, twenty-two dancing ladies, and twelve leaping lords; in all three hundred and sixty-four articles, one for each day in the year save one. This piece is now printed for the first time in a collection of carols.

FESTIVE CAROLS

HE first day of Christmas
My true love sent to me
A partridge in a pear-tree.

The second day of Christmas
My true love sent to me
Two turtle-doves and
A partridge in a pear-tree.

The third day of Christmas
My true love sent to me
Three French hens,
Two turtle-doves, and
A partridge in a pear-tree.

The fourth day of Christmas
My true love sent to me
Four colley birds,
Three French hens,
Two turtle-doves, and
A partridge in a pear-tree.

The fifth day of Christmas
My true love sent to me
Five gold rings,
Four colley birds,
Three French hens,
Two turtle-doves, and
A partridge in a pear-tree.

AND SONGS.

The sixth day of Christmas
My true love sent to me
Six geese a-laying,
Five gold rings,
Four colley birds,
Three French hens,
Two turtle-doves, and
A partridge in a pear-tree.

The seventh day of Christmas
My true love sent to me
Seven swans a-swimming,
Six geese a-laying,
Five gold rings,
Four colley birds,
Three French hens,
Two turtle-doves, and
A partridge in a pear-tree.

The eighth day of Christmas
My true love sent to me
Eight maids a-milking,
Seven swans a-swimming,
Six geese a-laying,
Five gold rings,
Four colley birds,
Three French hens,
Two turtle-doves, and
A partridge in a pear-tree.

FESTIVE CAROLS

The ninth day of Christmas
My true love sent to me
Nine drummers drumming,
Eight maids a-milking,
Seven swans a-swimming,
Six geese a-laying,
Five gold rings,
Four colley birds,
Three French hens,
Two turtle-doves, and
A partridge in a pear-tree.

The tenth day of Christmas
My true love sent to me
Ten pipers piping,
Nine drummers drumming,
Eight maids a-milking,
Seven swans a-swimming,
Six geese a-laying,
Five gold rings,
Four colley birds,
Three French hens,
Two turtle-doves, and
A partridge in a pear-tree.

The eleventh day of Christmas
My true love sent to me
Eleven ladies dancing,
Ten pipers piping,

AND SONGS.

Nine drummers drumming,
Eight maids a-milking,
Seven swans a-swimming,
Six geese a-laying,
Five gold rings,
Four colley birds,
Three French hens,
Two turtle-doves, and
A partridge in a pear-tree.

The twelfth day of Christmas
My true love sent to me
Twelve lords a-leaping,
Eleven ladies dancing,
Ten pipers piping,
Nine drummers drumming,
Eight maids a-milking,
Seven swans a-swimming,
Six geese a-laying,
Five gold rings,
Four colley birds,
Three French hens,
Two turtle-doves, and
A partridge in a pear-tree.

CHRISTMAS CAROL TUNES.

CHRISTMAS CAROL TUNES.

Carol for Christmas Eve.

The Lord at first did Adam make Out of the dust and clay, And in his nostrils breathed life, E'en as the Scriptures say; And then in Eden's Pa-radise He plac-ed him to dwell, That he with-in it should remain To

CHRISTMAS CAROL TUNES.

CHRISTMAS CAROL TUNES.

On Christmas Day in the Morning.

I saw three ships come sailing in on Christmas day, on Christmas day, I

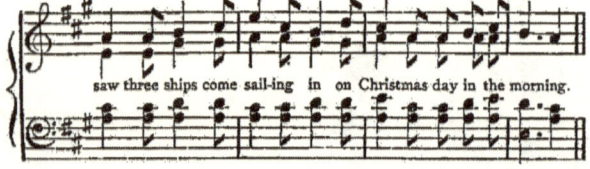

saw three ships come sail-ing in on Christmas day in the morning.

CHRISTMAS CAROL TUNES.

God rest you, Merry Gentlemen.

God rest you, mer-ry gen-tle-men, Let no-thing you dis-may, Re- member Christ our Sa-vi-our Was born on Christmas day, To save us all from Satan's pow'r, When we were gone a-stray. O ti-dings of com-fort and joy, and joy, O ti dings of com-fort and joy.

CHRISTMAS CAROL TUNES.

Remember, O thou man.
The original vocal harmony as published in 1611.

CHRISTMAS CAROL TUNES.

The Cherry-tree Carol.

Jo-seph was an old man, And an old man was he;

And he mar-ried Ma-ry, The queen of Ga-li-lee.

CHRISTMAS CAROL TUNES.

Carol for the Epiphany.

CHRISTMAS CAROL TUNES.

Carol on bringing in the Boar's head.

Annually sung at Queen's College, Oxford.

The boar's head in hand bear I, Bedeck'd with bays and rosemary, And I pray you, my mas-ters, be mer-ry Quot es-tis in con-vi-vi-o.

Chorus.

Ca - put A - pri de - fe - ro Reddens lau - des Do - mi - no.

CHRISTMAS CAROL TUNES.

Gloucestershire Wassailers' Song.

Wassail, wassail all o-ver the town, Our toast it is white, our ale it is brown, Our

bowl it is made of a map-lin tree, We be good fellows all, I drink to thee.

CHRISTMAS CAROL TUNES.

All you that in this house be here.

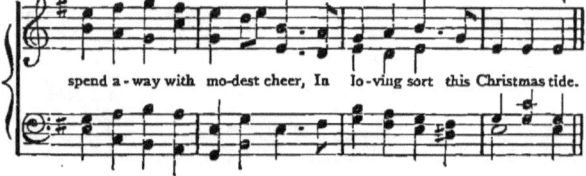

INDEX.

	Page
BABE is born	52
A bone God wot	132
A jolly Wassail-bowl	147
Alleluia now sing we	129
All under the leaves	105
All you that are good fellows	145
All you that are to mirth inclined	20
All you that in this house be here	170
All you that to feasting and mirth are inclined	165
An earthly tree a heavenly fruit it bare	18
Angel Gabriel (The)	68
A New Dial	107
Approach of Christmas (The)	175
As I passed by a river side	97
As I sat on a sunny bank	24
As I sat under a sycamore tree	24
As it fell out one May morning	91
As it fell out upon a day	95
At the beginning of the meat	118
A Virgin most pure	30
Babe of Bethlehem (The)	70
Be merry all, be merry all	180
Be we merry in this feast	54
Birth of Christ (A Carol of the)	10
Boar's head (Carols on bringing in the)	115

INDEX.

	Page
Candlemas Day (Carol for)	161
Candlemas Eve (Carols for)	159, 160
Caput Apri defero	119
Carnal and the Crane (The)	97
Cast off all doubtful care	18
Cherry-tree Carol (The)	58
Christmas Cheer	176
Christmas Customs	154
Christmas Day (Carols for)	16, 18, 19, 38, 127
Christmas day in the morning (On)	24
Christmas Eve (Carols for)	3, 154, 155
Christmas is my name	161
Christmas's Lamentation	161
Christo paremus canticam	53
Come, behold the Virgin Mother	70
Come, bring with a noise	154
Come guard this night the Christmas pie	155
Come, rejoice all good Christians	65
Contest of the Ivy and the Holly (The)	131
Dives and Lazarus	95
Down with the rosemary and bays	160
Down with the rosemary and so	159
Epiphany (Carols for the)	79, 82
From Virgin's womb this day did spring	16
Give way, give way, ye gates	143
Gloucestershire Wassailers' Carol	150
God bless the master of this house	137
God rest you merry gentlemen	27
Hark! all around the welkin rings	74
Here comes Holly that is so gent	129
Here we come a wassailing	152
Hey, hey, the Boar's head is armèd gay	116
Holly and Ivy made a great party	128
Holy Well (The)	91

INDEX.

	Page
How grand and how bright	36
I am here, Sir Christ-his-mass	127
In Bethlehem, that noble place	54
In friendly love and unity	43
Innocents (Carol of the)	45
In the reign of great Cæsar	56
I saw three ships come sailing in	24
I sing not of Roman	121
It is the day, the Holy day	38
Ivy chief of trees it is	130
Joseph was an old man	58
Joyful sounds of salvation (The)	56
Joy to the world, the Lord is come	73
Kindle the Christmas brand	161
Lulla lullaby, my sweet little baby	49
Make we mirth for Christ His birth	8
Man's Duty	109
Mark this song for it is true	45
Miracles of Christ (The)	104
Mortals, awake, with Angels join	76
My heart of gold as true as steel	134
Nay, Ivy, nay, it shall not be	131
New Dial (A)	107
New Year's day (Carol for)	78
Noël, Noël, tidings good	124
Noël, Noël, who is there	127
Now Christmas day approaches near	175
Now Christmas time is coming on	176
Nowell, el, el, now is well	52
Now is Christmas i-come	79
Now, now the mirth comes	156
Now that the time is come	174
Now thrice welcome Christmas	172
O God, that guides the cheerful sun	78
Old Christmas returned	165

INDEX.

	Page
On Christmas day in the morning	24
One God, one Baptism, and one Faith	107
One God there is of wisdom, glory, might	109
O you merry, merry souls	178
Partly work and partly play	158
Po, po, I love brawn	118
Rejoice, rejoice with heart and voice	16
Remember, O thou man	32
St. Distaff's day	158
St. Stephen's day (Carols for)	40, 43
St. Stephen was a clerk	40
Seven Virgins (The)	105
Sinner's Redemption, (The)	20
So now is come our joyful'st feast	138
The Angel Gabriel from God was sent	68
The approach of Christmas	175
The Babe of Bethlehem	71
The Boar his head in hand I bring	116
The Boar is dead	125
The Boar's head in hand bear I	120
The Boar's head in hand bring I	119
The Boar's head that we bring here	124
The Carnal and the Crane	97
The Cherry-tree Carol	58
The Contest of the Ivy and the Holly	131
The first day of Christmas	181
The first day of Yule	8
The first good joy our Mary had	87
The first Noël the Angel did say	82
The golden time is now at hand	10
The holly and the ivy now are both well grown	85
The Holy Well	91
The joyful sounds of salvation	56
The Lord at first did Adam make	3
The Miracles of Christ	104

INDEX.

	Page
The moon shone bright	62
The most worthy she is in town	130
The Seven Virgins	105
The Sinner's Redemption	20
The three kings	79
The twelve days of Christmas	181
The twelve good joys of Mary	87
The Virgin and Child	13
The Worcestershire Christmas Carol	36
This day Christ was born	18
This endris night I saw a sight	13
Tidings I bring you for to tell	117
Twelfth night Carol	156
Virgin and Child (The)	13
Wassail Songs	143, 147, 150, 152
Wassail! Wassail! all over the town	150
Welcome be Thou, heaven's king	6
Welcome, merry Christmas	180
Welcome, Yule	6
When Christ was born	53
When Jesus the Lord	104
Worcestershire Christmas Carol (The)	36
Yule-tide Carols	6, 8

CHISWICK PRESS:—PRINTED BY WHITTINGHAM AND WILKINS,
TOOKS COURT, CHANCERY LANE.

www.ingramcontent.com/pod-product-compliance
Lightning Source LLC
Chambersburg PA
CBHW021840230426
43669CB00008B/1026